Joining the Street People:

Henrique's Encounter With the Trinity

*Translated from Brazilian Portuguese
by Alphonse Gerwing*

ISBN 1-896971-12-1

October 2001

Printed by:
St. Peter's Press
Muenster, S
Ca

Dedication

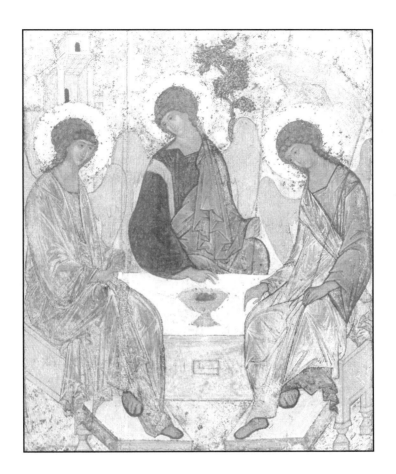

Icon of the Trinity by Andrei Rublev
(c. 1400)

This icon is generally considered the peak of Russian iconography. Icons in the eastern tradition are treasured like the Scriptures as revelations of the divine presence.

Beginning with Abraham's three visitors (Genesis 18 — the three often become "Lord" in the text), Rublev gives a magnificent visual lesson about the life of our trinitarian God. The three angels, "men" in the text, are invited to rest and eat. Notice the circular rhythm. Divine life flows from one to the other, inviting us into this circle of eternal youth and beauty.

Each person has a staff. They are travellers coming to earth, coming to live among us. On the table is a dish with the head of a calf, representing all those sacrificial animals leading up to Christ, the Lamb of God, seated at the right, his head bowed in acceptance of the divine will to give his life for humanity. In the middle the Father, with no suggestion of maleness as with the other persons, points to the cup of sacrifice. On the left is the Paraclete, the Spirit Helper, looking at the Son with infinite compassion and love. All is gift. All is love poured out for a world given infinite value by the God who comes to save.

"The icon of the Trinity is the most powerful image of inclusion," says Myroslaw Tataryn, Eastern-rite priest and professor of Religious Studies at St. Thomas More College, Saskatoon, Saskatchewan. "There is room there for you too."

This is the icon which Henrique refers to frequently in his letters and which accompanies him wherever he goes. This divine presence is visible, watching, when he enters into prayer, alone or with his street friends.

Fr. Lawrence DeMong, OSB

Introduction

Reading the letters of Henrique, Pilgrim of the Trinity, was a great joy. Barely into the prologue I already felt the need to share his odyssey with many readers.

This pilgrim of our own time carries on a tradition hallowed by Russian pilgrims for centuries. It is also in the tradition of Francis of Assisi, whose poverty and whose love of God and of the whole human family Henrique mirrors.

Besides showing us a Francis of our age, Henrique also incarnates the spirit of Dorothy Day, a woman who trembled with indignation at every injustice.

It's a fascinating combination at work in our pilgrim: a life of profound prayer so closely knit to solidarity with the world's discards (who, unfortunately are the majority!) that prayer and action become one.

And, though he joins no "movimentos," no organizations to struggle for a life of dignity for the poor, yet his spirit, like yeast in dough, is giving social activists everywhere new life, life which is grounded in the mystery of the Trinity.

In the multitude of "encontros" each day, year in year out, it is the self-revealing and the self-sharing of the Triune God that Henrique imparts.

The Portuguese word "encontro" cannot simply be translated by "encounter." Henrique describes "encontro" as "gift and welcome; it is sharing and communion. A genuine meeting becomes a parable of the mystery of the most sweet Trinity, an invitation to be seated at the table of the great encounter with the three sojourners that Abraham met and welcomed."

My hope is that the Pilgrim's letters to the world will be read and discussed in small groups everywhere in the English-speaking lands.

I hope that parish ministers in particular will use these letters in their monthly or weekly meetings as a springboard for prayer and for life-giving action in the community. Were that to happen then many of the complaints about parishes would vanish. No longer would those who "tremble with indignation over every injustice" have reason to say their parish is a do-nothing and therefore useless. And no longer would traditionalists say of those who try to carry the gospel into the marketplace, "but they don't pray!"

Henrique concludes a set of three letters in which he relates the work of three Brazilian groups as examples of many: a small religious community in a big-city slum; an alive parish in a drought-stricken small town of the Northeast; and a group of young people ministering to people in difficulty:

"Jesus is here, the Kingdom is being born. The church is living here a new spring, the hope of tomorrow. The signs are small and fragile, just a little handful of men and women of faith in the midst of multitudes, in a slum of 30,000. But that's how the signs of the Kingdom are: humble, simple, even 'innocent.' If the eyes of our souls could capture these signs, each a tiny flame of hope, then the five continents would light up with thousands upon thousands of these lights, each a springtime flower, a sign of the Resurrection."

Go with joy little book, just as does the Pilgrim, and help us see the "tender Trinity" as Henrique does, and to love all people in genuine charity, marked by welcome and sharing.

This hymn for Lauds in the church's liturgy expresses well what Henrique is about:

> Amid our anxious cares today,
> We praise you, Father, for the word
> Revealed in Christ, our daily bread,
> Who make our life your sacrament.
>
> In prayer we ask the help of grace,
> Your Spirit's life inspires our love,
> As pilgrims now we onward move
> The way Christ walked to bring good news.
>
> Our efforts hymn our rising hope,
> Your kingdom's glory in us dwells.
> May we be one in lasting love
> And sing your praise eternally, Amen.

Alphonse Gerwing, translator

Notes

Benedict Joseph Labre —

After having tried his vocation in monasteries over a period of three years, Benedict Joseph Labre, born in Amettes, France, in 1748, became a pilgrim. He was 22, and for the next thirteen years he journeyed on foot all over Western Europe. His final days were spent in Rome, living on the streets, sharing the life of beggars. On the Wednesday of Holy Week, 1783, he began his final pilgrimage, a journey that carried him to full intimacy with God whom he had desired so ardently and sought so long.

The Northeast —

Ten states comprise the region known as Brazil's Northeast. Though it is the size of Western Europe, this region has only one-tenth of Europe's population. The Northeast is rich in resources, though most of its population lives in abject misery, especially in the coastal zone, much of which is planted to sugar cane.

The people, the "Nordestinos," are a blend of indigenous, black and white races. Though slavery was abolished over one hundred years ago most Nordestinos today live in virtual slavery, excluded from the economic, social and political life of the country.

The Sertão —

The word "sertão" means "big desert." It's not desert as in the Sahara, but a semi-arid region that becomes desert from time to time when the rains fail. The sertão is the vast interior of the Northeast. Its droughts are frequent and sometimes prolonged. Isolation and drought have forged a toughness in the "sertanejos" that is legendary. The sertão is the home of Brazil's authentic folk culture: epic stories, improvised poetry played to the guitar and accordion, bandits like Lampião (Lightning) and his Maria Bonita. It is also the home of heroic figures with Utopian visions: Padre Cicero and his protegé, Padre Ze Lourenço; of the layman, Antonio Conselheiro. The movements led by these men have invariably been suppressed to protect "law and order," meaning the interests of the wealthy and powerful.

Much of the population of São Paulo (nearly twenty million!) is composed of expatriates from the sertão, fleeing drought, expelled from the land, or simply drawn to the big city.

League —

The author uses the term "league" frequently. It's a unit of distance much used in the sertão. It measures how far a person can walk in one hour, therefore, six kilometers or four miles.

Old Chico —

Affectionate nickname for the Rio São Francisco, majestic artery of the Northeast.

Palma —

A domesticated cactus, thornless, used as cattle feed in times of drought.

Canudos —

In the 1890s Antonio Conselheiro and 30,000 followers built Canudos, a city of hope, in the Bahian wilderness. Canudos defeated the first three armies sent against it. In 1897 Brazil laid seige once more to this seemingly impregnable city of the poor. Canudos never surrendered, but was demolished house by house until its last defenders died. Readers may wish to obtain Mario Vargas Llosa's epic novel about Canudos: <u>The War of the End of the World</u>.

Quilombos —

Through most of the seventeeth century the Dutch were attacking Portuguese settlements up and down the coast of Brazil. Many slaves took advantage of this turmoil to escape from the coastal plantations into the interior, creating free communities called Quilombos. The Quilombos were loosely connected and became very prosperous, even trading with coastal settlements. Once the Dutch were driven off the Portuguese attacked the Quilombos. The last redoubt, the Serra da Barriga, defended by the great warrior Zumbi, fell in 1692. Zumbi's head was cut off and paraded in the streets of Recife to warn any other slaves looking for freedom.

Winter —

The Northeast has two seasons, the dry and the rainy. With the rains come cool days which is, for the tropics, a "winter."

Punctuation —

Henrique's use of dots is an attempt to convey the disconnectedness of conversation and thought.

Pilgrim of infinite spaces

"Roberto, my little grandpa. . ."

Letter to Roberto

Island of Itaparica, Bahia
January, 1997

"God, creator of heaven and earth,
I thank you for your immense love.
I want to love you today and all the days of my life."
Benedict Joseph Labre

Roberto, this prayer was written by a pilgrim, Benedict Joseph Labre, "Pilgrim of the Absolute," but it could well have been written for you.

You two both came from the earth, our "Pacha Mamma" as you were wont to call her in the Quechua tongue of the Andes, your indigenous roots. He from the hills of Amettes, in France; you from the mountains of Cochabamba, in Bolivia.

You were both solitary beggars on the streets: he in Europe, you in Latin America.

You both played with the street children: he in Rome, you in Santa Cruz de la Sierra.

Both of you were mistreated and despised, rejected and humiliated, the way one despises and humiliates anyone who has just the sidewalk for a home, and cardboard for a roof. You both travelled through the same dark night: the night of the street.

You were both men of prayer, beginning and ending your day in a church: he in Santa Maria dos Montes, in Rome; you in the cathedral of Santa Cruz de la Sierra, before the same Jesus present in the tabernacle.

Both of you lived the same life of a pilgrim, a life that brought each of you from fear to the love of God that knows no limits.

Today I know it: your souls were twins.

Roberto, do you remember your first encounter with Benedict Joseph

Labre? It was the day when you came to the table of Love and of Communion with the most sweet Trinity. Our Father invited you to be seated in the first places, and you had to cross the room in front of everybody, almost not able to manage it, humble and simple as you are. But there, when you found your place, sitting beside you was a man who looked like you with that same radiant look, that same luminous smile, and so happy to welcome you! It was he. It was Benedict Joseph!

Roberto, I wrote a little of our story, revealing some of our secrets; you will forgive me if I was indiscreet. I told a little also about our companions: about Maria Flor, whom you taught me to love; our little street friends, especially Lazarus who slept with us one night, do you remember? And of Simon whom you loved with an affection so tender. . . .

Roberto, I am writing these poor lines as a homage to you. I owe you so much — I received so much from you.

May your memory never be obliterated from the earth.

Pray for me, for I have not yet completed my earthly pilgrimage.

Your companion as always,
Henrique

Roberto, gift from God. . .

Santa Cruz de la Sierra
August to October, 1989

The first night

Santa Cruz de la Sierra. . . . A city that's already become important, the second of Bolivia, located in the Amazon forest zone of this mountainous country. . . .

I arrived here on Thursday of last week. I caught a ride on a freight train coming from Puerto Suarez on the Brazilian frontier. Thirty-six hours sitting, sometimes lying on construction iron in a car open to all the winds. Thirty-six hours instead of the twelve hours it would have taken by passenger train. . . . But, God be thanked, I had no more money!

I spent the first night in a storage shed where they let me sleep. On Friday, at dawn, I walked to the city center, not knowing really where it might be but with an inner and intimate certainty about what I was soon to experience.

I looked for an open church and my steps led me to the cathedral. I arrived very early and spent the whole day meditating on the passion as related in the four gospels, meditating in silence on the mystery of the Trinity in front of the eucharistic presence, offering up this burning within my heart, listening to what an inner voice was telling me, pointing out a path as yet unknown to me. An irrational joy took hold of me — and continues still — stirring the depths of my soul. I felt like a child overcome in the face of a marvel too great to comprehend.

I didn't notice the night descending on the city and enveloping the cathedral. I only took notice of the time when, at six o'clock, the celebration of the eucharist began. I took part, making of it my final oblation.

Leaving the church after mass I felt extraordinarily free. Free and resolved. In my pack-sack I had a bible and a blanket. That's all. I gave the beggars seated on the cathedral steps my last coins, coins I had earned the evening before, helping unload the freight on which I had ridden. The last of the coins fell into the hands of an old blind man.

So, now I had nothing left, no security whatever. But I had an inner certainty of this marvellous call. In the cold and in the night of this city still unknown to me, everything seemed luminous, warm, beautiful. God's grace seemed to be enveloping everything, covering everything.

I remained standing below the steps for some moments. Then the old blind beggar addressed me: "Thank you," he said. "And where are you going to go now?"

"I don't know," I murmured.

"So then sit down here and let's talk."

I sat down, two steps below him. I held out my hand for alms. . . , the first time in my life. I actually received a few coins that night! But I had firmly resolved never to keep either money or food with me from one day to the next, like God's people in the desert, so as to live — even in material things — in complete trust in what the most sweet Trinity was calling me to live spiritually, namely in total confidence. To hope for all from the Trinity and from the Trinity to receive all. My only trust, my only security, my only hope would henceforth reside there. To have nothing more of my own, not even the power of counting on my personal resources. To that end, I handed on the coins to my blind companion as soon as I received them.

And he talked! Spanish mixed with Quechua, the indigenous language of Bolivia which I didn't understand very well. We sat there talking and begging until the cathedral closed at 8 o'clock.

Then Roberto, for that was the blind beggar's name, said, "So now, where are you going to sleep?"

"I don't know, Roberto."

"Well then, come along to my house."

His invitation created a problem of conscience for me. I had resolved to sleep on the streets that night, not of course having any idea as to how I would manage it, but with an inner certainty that this was my path, the way to which I was being called. And now, here was this man inviting me to sleep in his house. It would be a poor house without a doubt, I reflected, but still "a house". . . . At the same time an inner voice was telling me:

"Who are you to select the way? Let God do the guiding through such chance encounters! In this meeting up with Roberto there is something of the mystery of the Trinity waiting to be experienced. Go in full confidence. Let the Trinity be your guide."

I went with Roberto. We rounded the cathedral and, as he was walking very slowly, I asked, "Is it far to your house?"

"No, quite near."

We kept on walking at his slow pace, stopping every fifty meters or so for him to rest. When we arrived at the palace of justice near the cathedral in the central square of Santa Cruz, a building with a large overhang, he sat down on the ground. I thought he was tired and asked again innocently, "Is it far to your house?"

"Far, nothing! We're there. . . ."

O, the tenderness of the Trinity! God asked of Abraham his son Isaac, as we are asked to give up our own resolves even though they be inspired, in order to receive these again as pure gift, just as Abraham received back Isaac. Thus nothing more may be ours, all belongs to God. It is a total giving, even of our very selves!

That's how I met Roberto. We spent a week sleeping there in his "house" on the sidewalk. We begged alms each morning at the same cathedral door, and at nightfall we met again in the cathedral square and walked, arm in arm, to our house. Our. . . . Already I feel quite at home! Roberto is a gift to me from God. . . . More than a present: he is God himself welcoming me to the street for my new life as a beggar. . . .

That first night one more surprise lay in store for me. We lay down after having spread our cardboard on the ground and I fell asleep at once. A little later I was suddenly awakened. A hand was touching my shoulder and a voice was saying, "Wake and eat!"

I raised my head. There was Simon, a youth who was employed at the cathedral and studied at night. I had encountered him during my day of prayer there. Simon had a pot of hot chocolate and some biscuits. But he had above all a smile on that pure face, an innocence that gave him a surreal quality.

That face, that smile, reminded me of the words of God's angel: "Rise and eat or the journey will be too much for you."

I sat up on the cardboard and accepted that unexpected supper. Roberto was used to these celebrations with Simon. A deep friendship united the two, and each night, returning from night school, Simon would bring him something to eat.

"For my Grandpa," Simon said, tenderly.

Night Prayer

Each night, about 8 o'clock, I meet with Roberto, the old, blind beggar, mistreated and very poor. This moment of encounter is always one of great joy. We meet also at moments in the course of the day and at each such meeting we have new things to tell each other. I may bring some oranges, he a bun. Together we go to the overhang of the palace of justice where we sleep. Roberto is good-humored, a man of charm. He tells jokes, not always in good taste, but which have us laughing as we walk.

It's a strange sight these nights in Santa Cruz, an old blind fellow with white hair and a young beggar happily walking together to their home, a bit of sidewalk on the city's central square.

Once we arrive at our overhang, we make our bed, covering the cold concrete with cardboard. We continue talking until Simon comes after classes. He always brings something hot to drink and some biscuits. It's the tenderness of the Trinity that is incarnated in this young man of pure heart. There is more than mere friendship between Roberto and Simon. The love of a grandfather for his grandson, and of the grandson for his grandfather shines through their words and actions.

Before we sleep we share a last moment, a highpoint of our day: prayer. Roberto had long had this custom of praying at night before lying down to sleep, and now we do this together.

On our cardboard we kneel in front of the scripture and the icon of the most sweet Trinity. I light a candle and take from my knapsack a cross made of two pieces of wood. Roberto embraces the cross with the same intensity as would St. Francis of Assisi. With his free hand he grasps the candle just below the flame. I think he does that to enjoy the heat.

Kneeling thus, and holding both the cross and the candle, he raises his sightless eyes to heaven. In this movement he seems to send up his whole body, rising as fragrant incense. And so Roberto, a living icon, thanks God for his day.

Even when he has eaten nothing, when he has been humiliated, when he has suffered both cold and heat, his prayer is entirely that of thanksgiving. That and an appeal to God to cure his eyes. What a lesson for us all, for all humanity. He lives the beatitudes.

We read together the next day's gospel and conclude with the Our Father.

Then comes the night. For Roberto the world is all darkness. He has no idea what hour it is and he often wakes at two or three in the morning and thinks day has broken.

Roberto, friend and father

We lived together thus for over two months, Roberto and I, and we became close friends. Apart from meeting each evening and sharing the justice building's overhang as our "house," we had other moments in common during the day. The night prayer, said kneeling on our cardboard before we slept, became a privileged moment of brotherly union.

As our friendship grew, we experienced a sort of complicity between us. We no longer needed many words to communicate.

I will illustrate this with a little story.

One Saturday night I was invited by a church base community to celebrate the eucharist with them on the outskirts of the city.

I don't normally accept such invitations because I reserve the evening hours as a time of sharing with those who suffer on the city streets. But this time I accepted and said to Roberto, "I'll be late tonight. After eleven. . . ."

He answered jokingly, "Go in peace. Our 'grandpa' gives you his blessing."

I felt truly sent by my "grandpa" and left with my heart at peace.

I came home later than I thought I would. After all, it is a great joy to celebrate with the CEB's, the base communities, and we talked for hours. When I arrived at the overhang it was already Sunday. Roberto was sound asleep. Quietly I arranged my cardboard and set up my little cross of two pieces of wood. It always kept watch over our sleep. Then I lay down, very tired. I had done all this quietly so as not to awaken Roberto.

But scarcely had I closed my eyes when a voice said, "Is that you, Henrique?"

"Yes, Roberto. I got home late. Go back to sleep."

"And our prayer? We're not going to pray?"

"Oh, Roberto, it's already one in the morning!"

"So! Does God keep a schedule? I was staying awake to pray with you."

And then and there, Roberto rose, knelt on his cardboard and, in a tone of voice that brooked no opposition, said, "Where are the cross and the candle?"

How good it is that there are still grandpas to teach the young ones to pray. . . .

Lazarus, Alexander and the little friends. . .

Santa Cruz
September and October, 1989

"My name is Lazarus. . ."

Wednesday night, returning from celebrating the eucharist with the Franciscans, I arrived at the cathedral square passing one of the most luxurious restaurants of the city. I noticed a little child asleep at the foot of the steps leading up to the restaurant. He seemed to be about eight years old and he wasn't one of the street urchins that I knew, not one of those who generally sleep here in the square.

As usual I first looked for water to drink, visited with some people on the street, but my thoughts remained with that boy. From where had he come? What was he doing here? My anxiety about him kept growing and an inner voice said that I couldn't leave him there. Instead of going directly to the overhang where I slept beside Roberto, I returned to the restaurant. The child was still there.

I tried to wake him. He was in so deep a sleep that this proved difficult. When he did awaken he was frightened. I spoke with him but he replied with mere gestures. He seemed lost, not knowing what to do.

It was a cold night, and I had already wrapped my blanket around me. The child was trembling, wearing only shorts and a T-shirt. I told him that I myself slept in the square, hoping to gain his confidence. I invited him to come with me and to share the blanket. After a moment's hesitation he agreed and got up.

We walked across the square. He took my hand, holding it tightly in a gesture of trust.

On the way I asked him his name. . . .

And this boy who was lying at the entrance to a luxury restaurant in the hope of receiving the crumbs from the tables of the rich, shivering from hunger and the cold, answered in a murmur scarcely audible: "My name is Lazarus. . . ."

"There was a rich man. . . . A poor man, called Lazarus, was lying at his door. . . ."

(Lk 16: 19-31)

Alexander

Alexander, a child of about twelve or thirteen, begs in the square with his mother. He begs sometimes on the cathedral steps where I do the same with Roberto, other times in restaurants, and even right on the street, sitting on the sidewalk.

Alexander is mentally wounded. He has little control of his movements, speaking mostly in a babble. Both his appearance and his reactions cause him to be rejected, as much by fellow beggars as by children who tease him mercilessly. In a way even by his mother, who is mentally ill.

It is two weeks since we met and became friends. Like any other child, Alexander likes to play. We've played together many hours on the street. It is great fun for him and for me too! At such times Alexander shows himself to be quick-witted and lively.

He lives with his mother in a little house hidden away at the bottom of a piece of neglected, abandoned land, some blocks from the cathedral. Sometimes his mother locks him in the house but he gets out through a window. Occasionally I've brought him back home.

One night, about dawn, I was awakened by Alexander shouting. He was in the square, surrounded by other young fellows, stripped to his shorts and painted all over with blue latex. It was a loud blue and he was covered with it from head to toe.

I don't know if he did it himself or if the children helped — everyone had his own version. But what was clear was that the others were taking advantage of his predicament.

I got up quickly and hurried to separate Alexander from his tormentors. Even though we were friends and he trusted me, I had difficulty calming him. His high-pitched cries echoed through the square and his violent, hysterical movements made it difficult to get near him.

The street children stopped bothering him and, little by little, Alexander calmed down. There was no way I could wash him here, so I had him put on his clothes and led him home. His mother was awake, desperate about her son's whereabouts and screamed at him when she saw him. She pushed him into the house and slammed the door on me. She gave me no chance to explain. . . . I stayed for a few moments fearing to hear Alexander being beaten. But his mother, too, was calming down and instead of scoldings I heard water running in the shower. I went back to the square but couldn't sleep.

In my heart, I felt the wounds — wounds caused by so much violence, so much exploitation of human beings by other human beings. Seeing so many mentally ill and mentally deficient on the streets, defenceless, and abused — abused by those considered "normal"! I prayed, offering up this suffering to the one who alone could carry it, laying it at the foot of the cross.

Today neither Alexander nor his mom have appeared here in the square. Perhaps I'll visit them this afternoon.

The wound in my heart is still smarting. And I still have blue paint on my hands, on my pants and shirt. It's a memento of something that ought not to have happened. It's a symbol, a communion.

My little street friends

In the cathedral square one meets quite a few street children. Some are shoeshine boys, others guard cars. These return home at night. But still others have only the sidewalks for their house and the shadows for company.

Friendship and a sort of complicity grew up between them and me without our having sought it. It came as a gift from God, gratuitously given. These first weeks I was spending a lot of time in the square reading and writing as now, or simply sitting there.

But I learned to my sorrow that beggars do not have the right to use public benches in chique downtown parks. . . . Several times a policeman came asking me for my documents, intimidating me, even warning me not to be caught there again. He humiliated me with long interrogations in full view of the public. Once I was even expelled from the park. To this day I don't know why.

I imagined myself to be far removed from these children's thoughts.

But one day I was given some bananas. When a shoeshine boy passed by I gave him one. In a flash I was surrounded by a dozen kids. "We know you," they said. "You beg at the church door. You are poor like us."

One said, "We have the same enemy: the police. We saw them mistreat you, too."

Without my having sought it, they gave me to understand that I was one of them, I was on their side.

From that time on we met every afternoon. Often we shared nothing but each other's presence. When I have something I share — fruit, bread, milk that a lady gives me from time to time on her doorstep where a number of mothers with babies come to beg. Our sharing is reciprocal. They always offer me something and they are expert at getting everything one can imagine. One day they proudly brought me some homemade candies typical of this region.

One Saturday I had received nothing the whole day and towards evening I met up with my little street friends in the square. I played dominoes with some of them on the ground; others chatted, telling their day's adventures; others simply played aimlessly. Suddenly two of them disappeared and shortly afterwards they reappeared with orange juice and a buttered bun. They told me, "It's for you. It's no good going without food the whole day. Take and eat. . . . "

Such delicacy! How they guessed that I had eaten nothing that Saturday only God knows. Probably it's a sensitivity acquired by those who have experienced the same privations.

But, to receive from these street children my daily bread was for me a visible sign of the tenderness of the Trinity which always envelopes us. Some verses of psalm 23 echoed in my heart:

> *"The Lord is my shepherd,*
> *Nothing shall I want.*
> *He lets me rest in fields of green grass*
> *and leads me to quiet pools of fresh water. . .*
> *You prepare a banquet for me*
> *and fill my cup to the brim."*
>
> (Ps 23: 1,2,5)

One afternoon on a particularly hot day, my little friends spoke of a river near the city, the river Pirai, where one could go swimming. They all wanted to go and so we decided to go early the next Saturday. Already on Friday, even on Thursday, the boys spoke of nothing else. What excitement animated our little group!

On Saturday (Oh, tenderness of the Trinity!) a lady gave us just what we needed: lots of bread, some fruit and from my own begging I received cheese and tomatoes. What an abundance! Our heavenly Father looks after us, as Jesus said.

And so we went to a place called Pirai Colony, some distance outside the city. From there to the river was a three kilometer walk through a region of great natural beauty. The place was really isolated, almost lost. Not a house in sight, no noise from traffic. Only the river, the Andes on the horizon, nature and ourselves. It was a bit of paradise after seven weeks spent entirely in the city center sharing in the darkness and the suffering of the streets.

The water ran fresh and abundant singing its song of joy. Our swim renewed our bodies, relieving them of the grime of the street and of the pain and suffering experienced there. In the heart of mother nature, bathed by our sister, the water, far from tar and asphalt, from pollution and noise, our bodies could be reborn and live.

The transfigured faces of my little friends clearly showed this rebirth. Their gestures were now less aggressive, their words more gentle, their eyes luminous and shining. Far from the world of oppression in which they lived, here they could be what they still are: children, simply children. Children who love to play, who like to laugh, who like to sit on a lap. Children famished for tenderness, for love.

And so we played in the water letting time look after itself. The sun passed its zenith, smiling down on us. Nature itself had joined our play, our celebration among friends, our party for us, the little ones.

We spread a white towel on the sand at the river's edge, placed on it all the food we had received, some flowers to symbolize the beauty of the day, and the icon of the Trinity most tender — an icon in which the Father, the Son, and the Spirit participated in our meal. In the face of this plenty received from God's goodness we thanked the Father for the beauty of the place, for having gathered us together, for the food.

One child asked a blessing from "the Father in heaven" on us and on all the street children of Santa Cruz. He added "that nobody ever again would die of hunger on the street."

Oh, blessed day! A privileged moment of celebrating and sharing, of communion. A great peace filled our hearts and it was with light and happy spirits that we returned to the city.

Maria Flor, violence and tenderness

Santa Cruz,
October, 1989

These last weeks of my life with Roberto in Santa Cruz de la Sierra were marked by the presence of a third person: Maria Flor.

Maria Flor showed up one morning at the cathedral door where I was begging alms with Roberto. Roberto and she already knew each other and he was glad to see her back. He welcomed her with great pleasure. Roberto's heart is as big as the sea.

But now I perceived the limitations of my own heart. Right from the start I found it hard to accept Maria Flor. She was always complaining of aches and pains, of tiredness, of weakness. It seemed she had room only for herself in her conversations. She didn't act negatively with me or with Roberto but she spoke aggressively and with violent gestures to the Quechua Indians begging alms with their children. At times Maria Flor allowed the rancor, the bitterness in her heart to explode over these women. She even hit one woman who had gotten an alms she thought should have been hers. I had to intervene to prevent a general brawl from developing. And each time I felt called on to defend the Quechua women I got angrier with Maria Flor.

But what bothered me the most was the impression I had that she was abusing the goodness of Roberto. As soon as she would meet up with him she would ask him for something to eat. And if he had nothing she would complain, practically demanding food from him as her right. If Roberto bought a cup of coffee or a tart, she would demand the same for herself.

Worst of all, she was so bold as to ask Roberto for money. Actually she got twice as much from begging as he did.

One day, irritated by her abusive attitudes I mentioned it to Roberto. He replied, good grandpa of everybody that he was, "No, no!! She suffers a great deal."

I agreed with him. Maria Flor's past has been one long history of suffering, of disillusionment, of despair. She is mentally deficient, an "innocent" or "simpleton" as society sometimes categorizes these people.

Rejected and abandoned, she was cast onto the street much too early, at the age when her child's body was becoming that of a woman. Pretty and credulous, at various times she put her trust in men not worthy of trust. One day she confided in me, "I don't know how many men have abused me."

Wandering from place to place, from hope to disillusionment, she lost herself in the slime of suffering that marks the street. Where her eyes had once shone, now there was violence and bitterness.

Her body, her attitudes, even her words were a cry for tenderness, for affection, for trust and consideration.

Perhaps it was because she showed all this so exteriorly, that I denied her any sign of the affection she was craving. For more than two weeks she followed me about clamoring for that which I could not give her.

Only at Roberto's side — O that good heart! — did she find attention and tenderness.

Some ten days after we first met, after having begged alms all morning, Maria Flor said, "I am so weak. I can't take it anymore. I need to go to a hospital. But I don't like it there. I'm always alone, always alone."

And she added with the honeyed voice she sometimes used, "Henrique, will you visit me?"

There was no escape from the question. Unwillingly I said yes.

I had said yes but a week passed and I hadn't gone. I was even relieved by her absence. But God does not forget. Praying with Roberto one night, eight days after Maria Flor had been interned he said, "Let us pray for Maria Flor, alone in the hospital."

There followed a pregnant silence and then he added, "So, Henrique, have you been to visit her yet?"

"Oh, Roberto," I replied, "it's been over a week now. She must have been discharged by now."

"No way! If she had been, she would surely have come here. We're the only ones who know she has been hospitalized. The only ones. And she's expecting you. It's easy to get there. Let me tell you. . . ."

He gave me detailed directions and we lay down to sleep. I hadn't yet resolved to go.

It was only the next morning, the day before yesterday, that, praying in the cathedral, Roberto's words echoed in my heart, "We're the only ones who know she's been hospitalized."

I dropped all my arguments, my good reasons against going. I let my rancor fall away and surrendered. I resolved to visit Maria Flor in the hospital.

Coming out of the cathedral I did not sit down on the steps to beg alms as I usually did. The Father was taking charge of this day. I spoke briefly with Roberto and off I went.

All I knew was her name, Maria Flor. Arriving at the hospital, I gave them the date of her internment. It proved easier to locate her than I had imagined. They told me right away at the reception desk in a voice heavy with suspicion, "She's in an isolation room."

Then my heart opened, quite suddenly. A pain shot through me like being struck by an arrow. For this public hospital, with wards of fifty or more beds, there must be strong reasons for her to be placed in isolation. I guessed it was not because of any contagious disease but because of her attitudes, her behavior. What must she have endured this whole week??

The attendants in her wing eyed me with distrust: "Visiting Maria Flor???" they asked me, as if it were an impossible request or at least surprising. They led me through endless corridors, crossing many wards. I had the impression we were going where no one goes, to some hidden room, a room forbidden.

Finally we arrived at the last door. It was locked. The nurse hesitated and asked me in a low voice, "Do you really know her?"

I found no words to reply but I nodded my head and she opened the door. The ceiling was high and the whole room was painted blue. Maria Flor was sitting quietly on her bed. She wasn't bound as I had feared. On the contrary, she seemed quite peaceful.

Surprise and joy illuminated her face and brought brilliance to her eyes. "Oh you came," she exclaimed. "You came to visit me."

Nine days she had spent alone in this isolation room, unable to come out, waiting for me, hoping for one who resisted to offer her friendship and tenderness. With hands joined over her breast and almost trembling she looked at me fixedly. Her eyes shone with a great intensity and a tear fell down her cheek. Her inner fountain, dry these many years giving her eyes that empty and, at times aggressive look, was now once more a spring of living water.

We spent the morning together. She gave me apples, bananas, and even managed to get an extra plate for lunch which we shared in her room. She asked for news, not only of Roberto, but also of others in the square, even the street children, for whom I used to think she had more hatred and jealousy than friendship.

I looked up the doctor who was looking after her. She told me that Maria Flor, above all else, had anemia, already advanced, and that she urgently needed at least three blood transfusions. The blood must be paid for and, for Maria Flor, who had nothing, this meant getting it from a generous donor. Since this hospital had no blood bank she hadn't received any transfusions these nine days. I asked what blood type she had. It was the same as mine and so I offered to donate without hesitation. We scheduled it for yesterday morning.

I gave blood in the morning and Maria Flor received it in the afternoon. I've donated blood a number of times but always anonymously, never knowing who received it.

But yesterday was different. For me it was as though I had given for the first time.

Lying on the cot I watched, or better, I contemplated the blood pouring out of my arm. I could feel it going — journeying to one who did not know how to love.

Blood is life. To donate blood is to donate life. And so God called me to give blood to a person to whom I had refused tenderness and love. He asked me to give her of my life.

Later I went to Maria Flor's room. We spoke only a little. I told her she was going to receive blood. She thanked me. And, for the first time I relented and hugged her. The ice melted inside me and watered my eyes.

I left in silence.

From other letters. . .

I visit Maria Flor every other day. The hospital is a good distance from the city centre for someone on foot, but I sing for joy. I know that the time spent with Maria Flor will be a time of tenderness.

On the way I look for flowers to give her. Her room is bursting into bloom.

Maria Flor has received the other two transfusions. Friends I made in Santa Cruz these months have opened their hearts to her story and to her needs. St. John says in his first letter, "If a rich person sees a brother or sister in need but closes his heart against them, how can the love of God remain there?"

Maria Flor has to stay in hospital several weeks more. A cure will be slow and she will need much patience.

She's still in her isolation room, now rich with blossoms. However, she's no longer locked in but can wander freely through the wards and the hospital garden.

Maria likes to sew and is good at it. She mended my shirt, something it badly needed, and spends her days sewing for other people in the hospital, for patients as well as workers. It's so satisfying seeing her occupied in this way. Grateful people give her presents. From a pretty piece of cloth someone gave her she made curtains. Posters brighten her walls and in her table drawer are biscuits, chocolate, fruit.

Her face is transfigured. The shine in her eyes illuminates all her expressions.

The violence that used to characterize her glances, her gestures, her attitudes, has given way to gentleness.

Maria Flor has come into bloom — the bloom of tenderness.

Farewell

Santa Cruz, the last Sunday,
October, 1989

Last Wednesday, at the end of our daily prayer, I informed Roberto of my imminent departure from Santa Cruz. Shadows of sadness crossed his face but he said nothing except a blessing, "Go, and may all be well with you. We will be united forever in prayer."

Later he spoke for more than a half hour about Cochabamba, his native city, the place where I was heading, telling me about their cuisine and the places I ought to see.

Reckoned by the gestures of his heart Roberto will be the first in God's Kingdom. At this moment, so difficult for him, his first thought is for the other person. I listened without speaking, drinking in his words, sweeter than honey.

During these two months we had never lunched together. Roberto guarded that space of time for himself. Yesterday he said, "Now that you are going away we'll have lunch together and the next day too. And it's I who am inviting you."

I replied that just Monday would be fine but he insisted so firmly that today, too, we are lunching together. Tomorrow will be with Simon. Roberto is calling it our farewell meal.

I'm taking my leave of others too. Yesterday it was goodbye to Maria Flor. She is still in the hospital. She was overcome, wept a little and said, "You know, it was from you that I learned to be tender."

Leaving the hospital it was I who was crying.

One thing worried me these last days. Roberto had complained often of being robbed at night. Blind and old, sleeping alone, he was a defenceless, easy victim for anyone shameless enough to rob such people. These two months however in which I slept with him it had never happened. Our nights had been tranquil.

Several times I had caught bits of conversation among the street children about having stolen from Roberto — how often, how much. . . . My heart pained me at such moments but I made no comment. Anyway this wasn't the appropriate time.

The day before yesterday, sitting in the square with the children, I told them that I would soon be leaving Santa Cruz. After their questions and remonstrations I made up my mind to tell them what had come to me in prayer these last days, to seek their help.

"You all know Roberto," I began, "the blind, old man with whom I sleep at the palace of justice. Well, sometimes unscrupulous young fellows rob him during the night. Now how can he defend himself? These boys

18

don't realize that the little they take from Roberto represents a lot for him. And also Roberto is afraid at night, not knowing what may happen when he hears footsteps close by. You can imagine his fright! You know very well what it's like sleeping on the street and the fear that sometimes comes. So try to imagine what it must be like for a blind person. Now wouldn't it be easy for you to watch out a little for Roberto — you can recognize when somebody intends to steal — then maybe you could. . ."

I didn't get to finish my sentence. One of the boys, the strongest, Wolfgang, the leader of the group, got up and said with authority, "Don't worry. From now on nobody is going to steal from Roberto. You can count on us."

Wolfgang — he was one of those who bragged about having "rolled" Roberto various times. I put my trust in him and in the others too, all of whom repeated the promises of their leader.

Last Sunday I experienced one of the most moving moments of my stay with Roberto. There was an afternoon mass for the aged and infirm at the Franciscans. I invited Roberto. It was not easy to convince Roberto that he was welcome to participate. Although he prayed everyday, at night on the street and by day in the cathedral, it was over twenty years according to him that he had not attended mass. He was expelled from the church more than once.

But for this Sunday he said yes. It was with great joy that I brought him to the convent of the Franciscans where I go to pray every day and where people know about Roberto. They welcomed him with so much attention that he immediately felt at home.

During the homily a great longing for Roberto to receive communion filled my heart. I know how he prayed in the cathedral, and kneeling at night on the ground there in that recess, hidden behind a pillar. I knew of the preferential love of our heavenly Father for him. But I knew also that he had never received at the Lord's eucharistic table, had never received in his wounded suffering body the sweet presence of Jesus. It was for Roberto that Jesus had come, had been offered up in bread and wine. I resolved to ask him, "Roberto, do you wish to go to communion?" "Oh, you don't know how often!!! But can you imagine the padre giving me communion! And it's so many years since I last confessed."

A silence ensued during which I tried to understand all that he was going through, the exclusion he felt when he began to live on the street more than forty years ago. Exclusion that reached even to the eucharist. Roberto, never losing his faith, traversing a journey few are ever called to travel, but never revolting against God, in fact, on the contrary thanking God at the end of each day. . . .

I recalled the words of Jesus,

> *"People who are healthy do not need a doctor but only those who are sick. Learn therefore what this means, 'I wish mercy and not sacrifice.' Because I came to call not the just, but sinners."*
>
> (Mt 9: 12-13)

I was about to speak when Roberto asked, "Is there a padre here to whom I might confess?"

"Yes, there is."

Roberto wanted to go at once and I took him. He knelt, hands folded on his breast as he always did when he prayed, and made his confession. Then we returned to our places. When the time for communion came, Roberto said, "So then, aren't you going to take me to receive?"

I took him. My heart was so light and so thankful for this great grace.

After the celebration there was a party: a cake and cold drinks for everybody. And the cake was chocolate, Roberto's favorite!

From Cochabamba, some days later. . .

After more than two months together, saying goodbyes was difficult, especially for Roberto. He said, "You are the first close friend in my life."

How much suffering lay behind these words from this seventy-two-year-old man! I was very moved. At the same time I felt God's strength in my heart and in Roberto's too, giving him the courage to endure. I know that various street people I came to know in Santa Cruz visit Roberto, especially the street children, formerly his tormentors, now his friends and protectors.

There was a farewell celebration in the square with these children, the square where we spent so many afternoons together. Friends from Santa

Cruz had given me sweets and cold drinks for my little street friends. We shared these with much joy. It was beautiful. . . .

I keep praying that they will become Roberto's guardians during the nights.

N.B. After a six-month absence, I revisited Santa Cruz. Roberto and I celebrated our reunion with great joy. One of the first things he said to me was, "You know, I've not been robbed once in all this time."

PART I

Pilgrim
of the roads

Walking along the roads of suffering humanity

"The joys and hopes, the griefs and anxieties of humanity today, especially of the poor and of all who suffer, are also the joys and hopes, the griefs and the anxieties of the disciples of Christ."
(Gaudium et Spes, 1)

From the entrails of mother earth there rises a groan, the groan of humanity. For each open wound, for each humiliated human being this groan rises.

This groan of pain, this clamor of suffering does not wait on schedules, on theory or thesis, still less on talks and congresses.

But every groan calls, every clamor makes an appeal. It calls for someone to be present, it appeals for conversion. It calls on us to offer our lives.

Walking with no possessions, naked and unprotected, as much in love as vulnerable, the pilgrim journeys through the night of this pain, this suffering. It is a plunge into the ocean of suffering humanity.

Reading this anthology of letters, it is good to remember that the only authentic Christian vocation is that which leads to the poor, to the sufferer, to the wounded. If every vocation is born in the infinite tenderness of the Trinity and returns there, it is good to remember also that every vocation is a discipleship, a following of Jesus, the poor one; Jesus, the servant of Yahweh; Jesus, the crucified; Jesus the risen.

In the sertão: drought, famine, exploitation

"God will make it rain again. . . and my husband will come back."

*Ceará,
October, 1992*

These weeks I've been pilgrimaging through the sertão of the Northeast, where the total lack of rain for two years is scourging both people and nature. For many days I've been walking under a scorching sun sometimes up to fifty degrees in the shade, with only dried and burned brush for vegetation. Nothing, absolutely nothing green in these desolate lands. The dugouts are long dry. Everywhere people dig wells deeper in the hope of finding water, precious life-giving water.

Hunger stalks every home and one can no longer count the children who have become its victims. A nurse in the sertão of Piaui told me that any cause of death will be registered except the true one. It is necessary to hush up the spectre of famine. There are clandestine cemeteries of children where new little crosses hidden among the dry brush appear daily. These are the cemeteries of the "little angels," as people call them, of those who ought not to have died.

How many men in this one year have left their desolate land in search of employment in the big cities? And how many of them will never return?

But these folk of the sertão are still standing upright, head held high, unbowed in the face of drought. They are drought-resistant like the mandacaru, this cactus that alone is green in these times. Do they not say that even five straight years of drought cannot kill it? Resistant like the mandacaru.

In the deep sertão of Ceará I visited again a little community of fewer than twenty houses some thirty kilometers from the chief town of the municipality. To get there, one has to leave the asphalt and, for some days, travel on dirt trails, choosing always the lesser ones as they lose themselves in the desert of the sertão. Far from cities through tiny hamlets ever more isolated, I journey through these immense abandoned lands, abandoned by nature as well as by people.

The first time I visited this particular community was last year, at nightfall. I was, in fact, lost. I had been walking for some hours without meeting anyone and not knowing what lay ahead of me. But, as darkness descended, I heard a dog bark, a sign of life, hope for an encounter. I hurried my steps then and soon found this little group of houses. I stayed at the first, where some people were enjoying the fresh evening air. I greeted them and asked for water. I had a raging thirst. The traditional "You've come! Sit down" greeting of Ceará put me at ease.

I stayed that night with Antonio and Ivanilde, a young couple with a daughter Rosemary whose birthday it was. In our prayer that night before the icon of the Trinity and the light of little lamps we sang Happy Birthday for her. It was touching!

Last week, journeying through this part of the sertão of Ceará, I was hoping to meet this family again. But my friend Antonio was no longer there.

He had gone south, to São Paulo, in search of employment. If not, they would all have died here of hunger. "I don't know when he'll return," Ivanilde told me, her eyes full of tears and her voice trembling. Some children were playing on the floor of the house, a floor of beaten and swept earth, their bodies emaciated from malnutrition, their skin covered with sores. Over a wood fire in the kitchen she was making a little soup in a clay pot for the evening meal. "It's water soup," they say hereabouts.

When the sun went down giving the heavens their evening splendor and cooling the air, Ivanilde, head held high, murmured almost in a whisper, "But God will make it rain again. The winter will be good. God is with us, he will not abandon us. He will bring back the rain and my husband — my husband will return."

If only we knew how to wait the way Ivanilde knows how to wait!

I recalled lines a Russian poet wrote to his wife when he went off to war:

"Wait for me and I will return. Wait for me when all the others will have grown tired of waiting, and I will return."

The author of the letter to the Hebrews says,

> *"To have faith is to be sure of the things we hope for."*
> *(Heb 11: 1)*

Eating cactus. . .
. . .or refusing a glass of water.

In the sertão,
June, 1993

In these dry interiors of the states of Brazil's Northeast, the drought prevails everywhere. Parched lands, empty dugouts, dry wells, animals and vegetation dying. . . . The drought rules and with it its fearsome travelling companion, famine.

One day in the high sertão of Bahia, journeying through these lands of desolation, I saw a little house, a poor hut of clay plastered over wattles. Beside it was a little plot of palma, a drought resistant cactus, the only green thing to be seen. It's used for cattle feed in times like these. Beside the house, three stones holding in the wood served as a stove. A clay pot on the fire told me that folks lived here.

I was thirsty and stopped for water. The lady of the house welcomed me with downcast eyes, suffering etched on her face and on those of her children, born "according to scale" as they say in these parts. While drinking the water I noticed that most of the cactus plants were cut. Given their poverty I was sure they didn't own cattle. Even one head of livestock is considered wealth here.

Striking up a conversation, I said, "So you're selling cactus for cattle, eh?"

"Selling, nothing! We're eating it."

The water stuck in my throat. I hadn't known people could eat cactus. She continued, "It's because last year the rains were weak. Our beans lasted only a short time. We weren't even able to keep any for planting. And with the drought continuing this year there's nothing to eat. Only cactus. We cook it and eat it."

Eating cactus! Back on the trail I could scarcely believe what I had seen and heard. I remembered how incredulous I had been seeing children in a slum in Ilhéus roasting cockroaches, or street people I had seen so many times looking for beans, already sour, in garbage dumps, competing with the rats; of both men and women in Aracaju fighting with urubu, scavengers, for the remains of a carcass. All of this has but one name: HUNGER.

Little did I know that this encounter with famine would be the first of many such. . . .

Some days later, already in the sertão of Alagoas, I saw a man approaching me on the dirt trail I was following, carrying a sack on his back. He was walking fast. Doubtless, a peddler, I thought. When he came abreast of me he wasted no time on greetings. Gesticulating wildly and speaking loud and quickly he said, "You're going there?! Don't! Don't go! Don't go there! They're all eating cactus. Yes, really — cactus! You have to be crazy to eat cactus. But I'm not crazy. I'm not an ox to eat cactus. There everything is dried up. There's nothing left to eat. I'm going to Penedo. Stay alongside Old Chico (colloquial term for the majestic São Francisco river). They say the drought hasn't reached there. They have water. There they have food. Careful, man! The trails are full of crazies. Eating cactus, eating cactus."

And so he went on his way muttering, "Eating cactus."

In the sertão of Bahia or Alagoas as well as in other states of the Northeast, drought and hunger have brought entire families to this: eating cactus! Cactus — cattle feed. But, when there is nothing else, the victims of drought and of society that spends little time worrying about it, have no recourse except to eat cactus as their daily bread. Their faces beaten and famished, and sometimes despairing as was this fellow I just met, reveal the harshness of the drought and how little the majority of politicians in this region do to ameliorate its effects. On the politicians' farms no doubt the cattle are still fat, feeding on rations, or, if bad comes to worse, cactus.

And yet, in the midst of all this suffering, I find welcome smiles, a cup of water, a bit of dry meal. "What we have is little, but we share," a man from the sertão told me once when he gave me a bit of meal with bean broth.

Another encounter showed me wealth can suffocate this natural and spontaneous generosity and even cause it to disappear entirely.

On leaving Bahia and entering Sergipe what a difference. Here wide, asphalted highways replaced the dirt roads. The many houses of clay and wattles with tiny cultivated plots around them, gave way to houses with porticos, painted in bright colors and set in vast fields. Here the hoe has given way to the tractor, and in place of small-holders, here were big farmers with hired help, with cowboys and day laborers in harvest time.

Without realizing how a simple state boundary could produce such a difference, I travelled on confidently. I had become accustomed to meeting many people on the roads of Bahia, and now I was confronted with the solitude of these infinite spaces, apparently without people.

I hadn't brought water with me and, under the hot sun of the sertão, I began to feel thirst. No house in sight! For two hours I continued, seeing only tractors planting beans. All belonging to the same owner. All the same farm! All the land I could see to my left, all the land to my right — one farm.

Finally I spied the owner's house in the distance and headed for it, eager for a drink of water.

The driveway was wide. I passed garages with more tractors and two cars; near the corral were machines to grind animal rations; farther on, a pump and an imposing water reservoir.

A dog ran toward me, barking, really threatening. I had to sue for peace. I remained quiet, talking to it, letting it sniff my hand, not knowing if it might bite. But the dog accepted me and that opened the way for me to approach the house.

I didn't need to call — a man was already on the porch, waiting. Doubtless, the owner.

"So — what?!"

I greeted him calmly, "Good day." I paused a moment expecting a reply but none came. I continued, "Please, sir, I've been travelling and I'm thirsty. Could I have a glass of water?"

Now the reply came immediately and these are his exact words: "Don't have any. No water. Be on your way."

I was surprised and alarmed, so nonplussed I began to stammer, "But sir, just a little. . ."

"Don't have any."

Clearly there was no point in insisting. Nor was there any use in pointing out that all about us were palm trees with coconuts filled with fresh sweet coconut water, or that the orange trees behind the house would provide fruit admirably suited to slaking thirst! I wished him a good day and continued on my journey.

It was the first time I was ever refused water.

These two meetings, that of the lady who had only cactus to feed her family but gave me a cup of water and this farmer saying, "We have no water," reminded me of James:

> *"God chose the poor people of this world to be rich in faith and to possess the kingdom which he promised to those who love him."*
>
> *(James 2, 5)*

Water and Cashews. . .

The exploitation carried out by the big land owners

In the sertão,
October, 1994

I left the sertão of Ceará in mid-September and journeyed here to the sertão of Paraiba through a succession of hidden, lost hamlets. During this month I encountered a great variety of places and experienced some really intense moments. Often I was welcomed without ever having to ask. Such meetings were always opportune moments for heartfelt sharing. Chance meetings on the roads, too. The people of the Northeast "carry their heart in their hand," as the saying goes.

On this month-long journey I saw the great extent of the people's suffering and the exploitation of which they are victims. Two episodes particularly stick in my memory.

In one community I passed through, men, women and children were going two kilometers to find the only potable water in the place. The local political strongman, owner of most of this region, had a dugout constructed on his farm with public money, very near his house where he didn't even live permanently! Perhaps he was wanting to admire the water from his veranda on leisure weekends and say, "How beautiful is this sertão!" Or perhaps it was his pious wish not to deprive his cattle of water at their convenience. . . .

But can he have forgotten that two kilometers away fifty families had no water to drink? Fifty families have to traverse those four kilometers daily and, on the way back, loaded with cans of water carried on their heads or on their shoulders. And can he have forgotten that his are not the only cattle in the sertão? Has he no heart?

Another day I skirted a huge cashew plantation — a walk of over four hours, a plantation belonging to a large industrial consortium in the Northeast. They were all lined up, these trees, thousands upon thousands of cashews.

When the sun was at its zenith and the day at its hottest I arrived at the house of one of the plantation's overseers. I asked for water and he welcomed me warmly. He gave me a glass of cold water and said, "I know what it is like travelling under this hot sun. I've done it often. And you must be hungry too. Rest during the heat and stay with us for lunch. It's only beans and meal but we share it gladly."

We ate in the shade of a cashew tree because the house, small and low, was very hot. His name was Raimundo, his wife Evinha. They had eight children from three years to fifteen. The meal became a veritable celebration.

Raimundo and Evinha told me what all they'd been through recently. They had no choice when the "boss" asked Raimundo to take charge of the plantations. He had had a job in the factory that the same consortium owned in the city. "It was this or lose my employment," he added.

And so here, far from everything, in a tiny house with a lean-to kitchen, they lived, ten people with two beds in the middle of thousands upon thousands of hectares of land.

Isolated from everything and from everybody — no transport and hence no schooling for their children. Here they live and work, the older children helping Raimundo with the cashews. He gets one half of a minimum salary because, says the boss, "You have the house free."

Near the end of the meal one of the many watchmen appeared. Mounted and armed, it's their business to guard the cashews especially those along the road to prevent thievery. They have orders to "shoot on sight," and, if they catch a thief they tie him to a tree until the next day. When one realizes that the plantation measures twenty-four kilometers by twelve kilometers, all planted to cashew trees one questions the need for so much policing. Some cashews fewer wouldn't harm their harvest.

(I calculated the plantation has 720,000 trees!)

This "ad hoc" militia, armed and given such orders, makes us question our society and the consequences of its economic policies.

In the bible we read of an owner of much land ordering his hired men at the harvest always to leave some ears of grain or some fruit on the trees for poor people to glean:

> *"When you harvest your fields, do not cut the grain at the edges of your fields, and do not go back to cut the heads of grain that were left. Do not go back through your vineyard to gather the grapes that were missed or to pick up the grapes that have fallen; leave them for poor people and for foreigners. 'I am the Lord your God.' "*
> *(Lv 19: 9-10)*

Ruth, the grandmother of David, the great king from whose family Jesus was descended — Ruth exercised this right and went to the fields to gather the ears left by the reapers because neither she nor her mother-in-law, Noemi, had anything to eat (Ruth 2).

But now the prevailing "law" seems to be greed, profit, income, egoism. And, to satisfy this "law" they tie people to cashew trees for a whole day, or they deprive an entire village of water solely for the benefit of their cattle.

The two situations reflect the same reality, that of exploitation of human beings by other human beings. The political system as much as its economic policies leads to such exploitation.

When will we build a society whose aim is to serve people and not to win more power and money? From so much suffering, from so many situations like these of exploitation and oppression, comes the cry of the people, a cry that rises to God, the God of Moses, who said to him:

> *"I have seen how cruelly my people are being treated. . . . I have heard them cry out to be rescued from their oppressors. I know their suffering and so I have come down to rescue them. . . ."*

> *(Ex 3: 7-8a)*

In the green hell of the cane lands

Pilgrimaging through the cane region — land of suffering and pain

The cane lands,
October, 1994

These last days I passed through a landscape once more clothed in green. I saw once more how the earth can flourish, producing its fruit to sustain the human family. I saw fields of manioc, corn and beans in abundance giving the fields a festive air.

It is the same rich earth of the tropics, blessed with abundant rain and with a climate favorable in every way that I've been travelling through this past month.

But what I have just crossed is the cane zone, so-called because it's all planted to cane. For three whole weeks, from Paraiba to the south of Alagoas I walked between cane and more cane, surrounded on all sides by cane, a prisoner of cane.

Cane right up to the asphalt! Cane on the heights, cane in the valleys. No more trees, no more legumes, no more flowers; nor any grain fields or gardens; and of course no forest! Only cane — the green hell of the cane country.

Hidden behind this intensive monoculture is the equally intensive oppression of an entire people. Just as the land was and is enslaved to produce exclusively cane, so also were and are the people enslaved to plant, weed, cut and treat the cane. The word "slavery" may have disappeared officially, but the reality it represents, remains. "Plantation owner" has disappeared too, but only to be replaced by "mill owner". . . .

The salary of a cane cutter depends on how much cane he can cut and tie into bundles of ten kilos each. The cutters I talked to were getting less than $2 U.S. for cutting 1,000 kg of cane! And many simply can't manage their daily "quota." Women and children, who are also pressed into service as cutters, are the first victims of such exploitation. Only the men are strong enough to cut a ton a day. But even they, working thirty-one days of the month, I don't know how many hours per day, under hot suns and heavy rains, in dust and humidity — even they will not receive as much as one minimum salary at the end of the month. How do they manage to live?

I had many encounters with these workers, and was able to learn about their lot at close hand; with cutters walking home on dusty roads, in hamlets where their families live, lodged in houses that are little more than match boxes; meetings in church communities, one of the few places where free expression is possible and an awakening of conscience can happen.

Travelling these weeks through all this cane and ever more cane I felt the people's pain in my heart, a tightness in my breast, a cry I could no longer hold in, a groan, and in prayer an intercession for this people enslaved in the green hell of the cane lands.

Coheleth, a Jewish philosopher who decided that he "would study and examine all the things that are done in this world," (Ec 1: 13) tells us:

> *"Then I looked again at all the injustice that goes on in this world. The oppressed were crying and no one would help them because their oppressors had power on their side."*
>
> *(Ec 4: 1)*

There is no one to console them! Who will hear the summons, the call of the Lord which resounded from the mouth of the prophet:

> *"Comfort, comfort my people."*
>
> *(Is 40, 1)*

Exploitation, yesterday and today

Pernambuco,
June, 1992

It's four days since I have seen only cane. Plantation after plantation. Four days through the cane lands of Pernambuco in the heart of the cane zone, always fenced in by cane. Right up to the edge of the highway but also to the very rails of the train track I followed for several days — all

33

cane, ever more cane. No forest, not even trees or grass. Only cane.

Between the towns of São Bento do Sul and Macaial, more than twenty kilometers, one didn't need to ask, "Who is the owner?" All belonged to the mill Frei Caneca. And here, around Rio Formoso, already near the coast, it all belongs to the mill, São André.

Frei Caneca belongs to one family. Thousands and thousands of hectares. All the land hereabouts. A whole fleet of their trucks passed me on the road, and when I come to a hamlet there is always the same view — one or more long, narrow buildings, divided door, window, door, window. These are the homes of the cane cutters. Little boxes strung out in a long line. Certainly cheap to construct! And it's equally certain that he who ordered their construction doesn't live here!

Those who do live here have no rights — no rights and no dignity. When house, land, football field and sometimes a little chapel or school all belong to the employer, what freedom do you have? And where can you go? As a prison it appears to be open but in fact, turn where you will, there is no exit from here. Here you stay, a prisoner of cane. Is this much different from the slavery of a hundred years ago?

I thought I was seeing here, at the end of the twentieth century, what Emile Zola described in the north of France at the end of the nineteenth, in the coal mines. When everything belongs to just one family: mines, houses, power, justice, money. . .and even hypocritical "charity," used to tranquilize the conscience. . . .

Do we have to repeat the errors of the past? Do those who rule through the power of money in this economy always have to crush those who work? Is all this suffering really necessary?

Whenever a truck carrying a load of cane cutters to or from Frei Caneca passed me, I greeted these men, but my heart was sorely afflicted. A hundred and fifty men, perhaps more, standing inside the cages of a cane truck carrying them to the cane fields, and at high speed. . . . That's the way to treat workers? That's respect for human beings?

"The crucified ones of the cane lands" — that was the theme of the first organized pilgrimages in the land of cane. Now I understand that this is no exaggeration. This is the reality.

Oppression and violence

Alagoas,
June, 1993

Night had already enveloped this little city in the interior of Alagoas. A fresh breeze made me forget the heat of the day, the sweaty journey. Even my weariness was ebbing. All those leagues under the hot sun left my arms burned and my feet sore. But tomorrow will be a new day, a new road, new encounters.

It's a week since I left Recife and Pernambuco. How different I find each state to be! If Bahia and Ceará are the most welcoming, Alagoas distinguishes itself by the social tension that reigns there. In the cane lands I am traversing these days all the land is planted to cane. I see no beans, no corn field, no manioc. Only cane. . . . Endless vistas of cane. Each five or six leagues forms one immense mill or plantation. The mill grinds the cane to produce alcohol, that famous substitute for gasoline, or sugar. The mill is a giant factory filling the air with a foul odor. It is "tiborna," the residue of cane. Discharged into the rivers it annihilates all life. How many rivers have been thus polluted and killed! And all about are the little dwellings of those who work here, that is to say, the slaves. . . . The same long, narrow buildings I saw last year in the cane lands of Pernambuco, the same inhuman architecture.

Tension everywhere. Like a law of silence. For one sensitive to his surroundings, to relations between people, this is painful. No one speaks (and one soon perceives that it is best that way) of the two Italian priests who had to flee because of threats and even of assassination attempts. In Paraiba, I received a letter that one of them wrote prior to leaving the parish. It spoke of violence, of oppression, of things one can hardly imagine to exist at the end of the twentieth century. It spoke of bodies burned, cut into pieces and scattered so as not to be identifiable.

In a burned patch that I passed yesterday all surrounded by cane, a young fellow in all innocence showed me where part of a burned body had been found last week. In the midst of this rich, red land of the tropics, in the midst of this cane, tall and green, this little spot of scorched earth cries out. On continuing my journey the great walls of cane, sometimes reaching heights of two and three meters seemed to me themselves to be oppressors.

Was I never welcomed in Alagoas? In place of the traditional "You've come!" or "Have a seat" of Ceará, here I am met with silence, a silence heavy with distrust, a silence that even a cheery "Good day" can't break. The air itself is charged with distrust, with silence.

No one speaks to anyone! Except Luís with whom I travelled for two days. He fled the drought two years ago, went to São Paulo, but because he found the cold there unbearable he is returning to his sertão. Without money, without hope. We conversed a good deal, but then Luís is from Paraiba.

"There's no school here — only cane."

The cane lands,
October, 1994

Late yesterday I met two children on one of these dusty roads walled in by cane: a boy of eleven and a girl of ten.

I saw them from far off. Carrying sickles on their shoulders, they walked slowly side by side. They didn't speak, they didn't sing; nor did they run or jump as children do. They walked like adults weighed down by an oppression that is too much for them.

They wore long-sleeved shirts, pants and boots. Though this adds to the heat and the humidity they must endure, it is necessary to protect the body from cuts from the saw-toothed cane leaves. Their faces, their hands, clothes and hair were all covered by charcoal and ash, ash from the previous night's burning of the dry lower leaves.

They had come from cane cutting.

The day had been long for me. I had travelled over six leagues through this green hell under a hot sun. My body was sweaty and tired. And I was hungry. But, seeing these two, I realized that what I was enduring was trifling in comparison.

The two had already come quite near but appeared not to see me. They kept their eyes fixed on the road but far off, on the horizon, beyond the cane, perhaps on another world — a world where they would have the right to be children.

Their bodies were rigid, inflexible. Only their legs moved: a cadenced regular movement, so regular that it no longer seemed human. Like automatons.

My heart felt constricted. The suffering of these children was crying out this evening and its cry reechoed in me. I must speak with them. I cannot pass by without reaching out with some compassion.

"Good evening," I greeted them.

They stopped. But they stopped the way they walked — like automatons. They stopped and looked at me. Mute.

"Good evening, children," I said, a bit more energetically.

Their eyes continued empty. No shine, no life. Their eyes, too, seemed covered by charcoal and ash. Their lips remained closed, unsmiling. Closed, unsmiling lips; dry eyes, devoid of sparkle; expressionless faces the colour of charcoal — I have to ask myself once more, to what are these children returning? A place without a name, a place beyond death.

I crouched so as not to tower above them and said, "You're coming back from work, right?"

Then the girl, the younger of the two, answered, "Good evening. We went to cut cane."

"And did you cut much cane today?"

"Lots. The whole day."

"But you're too young for this, aren't you?"

"Yes, but it's necessary. For not to die."

"To not die? You mean from hunger?"

"No, not from hunger. It's — it's that the owner of the mill ordered us to cut. He wants everybody to cut. We have to obey, otherwise. . ."

I closed my eyes, and found no more words. I remembered the stories of people disappeared; of bodies burned and scattered so as not to be identified. I remembered a man I had met a few days earlier, hidden by some church people. Dismissed from a cane mill, he had asked for his rights. The owner of the mill ordered the police to seize him. At the police station he was tortured, then taken to a cane field where he was shot and left for dead.

But he wasn't dead and hid out like an animal, wounded and hunted. With the support of organizations connected to the church he launched a lawsuit against the owner. But, on account of this, he now has to live in hideouts, a refugee, in permanent danger of being caught and killed.

The violence and oppression of the cane lands is beyond imagining.

My strength failed me and I sat down on the ground. The children remained standing in front of me, rigid. The sun was almost set, the sky a luminous orange and red. The contrast was stupefying: the resplendent heavens and these two children, the color of charcoal.

It seemed necessary to me to change the subject, to move from death to life. I needed to speak to children as a child — to speak of the dreams of children. We tried to talk for awhile about everything and nothing. Gilza spoke more than her brother, Cireneus. Cireneus — prophetic name. This boy of twelve with this name was carrying a sickle on his shoulder to cut cane, as his namesake, that other man of Cirene carried Jesus' cross.

In talking, he let slip, "We can't study, no."

"You can't? Because of work?"

"We just can't."

He was silent a moment, but the silence hid something. I didn't feel it was right to pry further, but Gilza explained. "You know, there's no school here. Only cane."

Gilza. . .only a little girl of ten, a cane cutter could express herself well using so few words and expressing so succinctly the reality of cane country: "Only cane here!"

Walking through the cane lands one hears the silent shout that rises from the entrails of mother earth. And the walls of cane along the roads remind us that oppression and slavery have not disappeared.

There's no school here.

No dignity either.

Nor is there liberty.

Only cane.

"They will never take over my land"

In the cane lands
October, 1994

Some days ago, travelling through this region where one sees only cane, suddenly I saw a hillside covered with jaca trees, mangos, bananas. A little island in this ocean of cane, an island of dark green in a sea of bright green cane. Coming nearer I saw it was a planted field. The manioc was already big, and the stalks of dried corn testified to the abundance of this year's harvest. There were also cashew trees, some pitangas, jambo and papaya. A little stream ran between the trees mirroring nature's joy. In the middle of this enchanted island was an old house of clay and wattles. It was rooted in the earth from which it was born, was one with it.

After so many days of seeing only cane this little plantation seduced me. My dry throat prompted me to ask for water: a pretext — but only partly! — for an encounter.

I clapped my hands and an old gentleman appeared. He gave me water and I praised the beauty of his field. It needed nothing further for him to tell me the story of this piece of land.

Manoel, for that was his name, was nearly ninety. He said that years ago there were a lot of small-holders hereabouts. But the local land and mill owner wanted to buy all these small holdings for cane. Pressure, threats, even violence brought all these families to heel, giving up their parcels of land for a portion of bread. They gave up the dignity of being workers for the slavery of cane cutting. They gave up the nobility of living on their own land for the humiliation of having to sell themselves for day work.

All the families did this except Manoel. He said he would never give up his father's farm, the land where he was born and grew up, where he had married and raised his family, the land that had given him the dignity of doing his own work.

The pressure from the mill owner intensified to the point of veritable persecution. They chased cattle onto Manoel's field, burned his crops three years running, knocked down his banana trees at night, even rerouted the little stream that watered and fertilized his acres.

The bank refused Manoel loans, loans to which he had a right as a rural worker. Bankers and mill owners walk hand in hand in these parts. Sometimes they are even one and the same person.

As to the mayor's office, it was no use for Manoel to expect anything from that quarter. With very rare exceptions the political power in the cane lands, whether municipal or state, is in the hands of the mill owners or dependent on them. And they use this power, not in the interests of the people, but to shore up their domination, their exploitation, the regime of slavery they have foisted on the people.

But they never overcame the resistance of Manoel, and they never will.

"While I live, and with the help of God," he declares, "never will they get my land." It's an affirmation that his oldest son, who lives and works with Manoel, makes his own.

There is a holy boldness in those who whatever the cost, refuse to bend the knee to oppressive power. It's the boldness of Mordecai before Haman (Esther 2); of Ananias, Misael, and Azarias before the great king, Nabuchadnezzar (Daniel 3); or of John the Baptist before Herod (Mark 6: 17-20). It's the life of Ghandi or of Margaret Alves in the rural struggle and of Santo Dias in the factories.

Note the hot indignation of Amos in this cry for justice:

> *"Because they sell into slavery honest men who cannot pay their debts, poor men who cannot repay even the price of a pair of sandals. They trample down the weak and the helpless and push the poor out of the way."*
>
> *(Amos 2: 6-7)*

Will we silence the promised restoration and the preferential option God made for the poor, the victims of injustice, which the same prophet announces?

> *"I will bring my people back to their land. They will rebuild their ruined cities and live there; they will plant vineyards and drink the wine; they will plant gardens and eat what they grow. I will plant my people on the land I gave them, and they will not be pulled up again — the Lord your God has spoken."*
>
> *(Amos 9: 14-15)*

In an ocean of bright green cane, this dark green island of jaca and mango trees speaks of resistance and of hope. As long as people like Manoel exist, humanity can move forward with head held high.

Who makes history is not the mill owner, it's Manoel.

Who is chosen by God are not those who "grind into the dust the heads of the weak." No, it is Manoel who "plants his garden and eats of its fruits," and who "will never be pulled up from the land."

Caldeirão (Big Cauldron)

Juazeiro do Norte,
September, 1991

Friday morning, very early, I set out from Juazeiro do Norte for Caldeirão, the place where the holy man, Zé Lourenço founded a community in 1926 at the request of Padre Cicero.

People from the sertão of the whole Northeast came there to work the land. There they found a little house to live in, a plot of land to cultivate. And, in the person of the holy man, Zé Lourenço, they found someone who respected them, someone ready to listen to them. There they found a place and room to express their faith — the simple but authentic faith of those who know the land. They constructed a chapel through a building "bee" and there they gathered for daily prayer with Zé Lourenço around the "Bom Jesus," the Good Jesus.

"Everything was owned in common," says Maria de Maio. She was born in Caldeirão and lived there until the age of sixteen. "Everything was green there even when the sertão had drought. Caldeirão had dugouts, rice fields, corn, beans, manioc. . . . Nothing was lacking."

During the severe drought of 1932 Caldeirão was the only place in the sertão of Ceará that stayed green and had plenty. Peasants came in thousands in search of food so as not to die of hunger.

The movement to Caldeirão reached such proportions that it began to worry those in power. Seen as a threat by the government, as a danger by the oligarchs of that time, Caldeirão was destroyed by the army in 1937.

Even planes were used against these peasant families of the sertão who had pledged themselves not to take up arms. . . .

It's a festering wound in the history of the Northeast and of all Brazil reminding us of similar events of the past, of the Quilombos, of Canudos. Is it really necessary that history thus repeats itself? Must blood always be shed, the blood of innocents, of those seeking a more just society?

Caldeirão is ten leagues from Juazeiro do Norte. Like the people of that time, leaving Padre Cicero in search of the promised land of Caldeirão, I set off walking through woods, along dirt trails not really knowing the way. After all, nobody goes to Caldeirão any more.

Moving from hamlet to hamlet, I reached Breia. At Breia one has to begin climbing the mountain ridge and houses are few. I mistook the trail several times and had to backtrack considerable distances. It was already dusk when I reached the top of the ridge. There were no more houses but there was a trail to the right. According to a man I had met an hour earlier, it was the path to Caldeirão. I took it. I walked on some thirty minutes, hearing nothing, seeing no lights. Darkness had already overtaken me, and I was lost. I retraced the trail and walked about an hour without seeing a single house although I did see some lights in the distance. I descended the entire ridge and down in the valley I finally met someone. I explained what I was looking for and he said, "Go back and before ascending the ridge there's a trail leading off this side. That will take you to Caldeirão; there's an encampment there. The chapel is nearby."

Confident and full of hope, I resumed my journey. Actually, I already knew that a group of landless peasants had occupied a part of what was once Caldeirão, and from far off I now saw their campfire. When I got there the people were all assembled around the fire for their daily meeting.

I approached and wished them good evening. All eyes were turned on me but no one spoke. I understood then that I had inadvertently come at an inopportune hour and that I was not welcome. The campfire could not thaw the icy atmosphere between us. A cold voice said, "Here we are all one family. We don't welcome people from the outside. We were expelled from Caldeirão by the padre who owns it. We were booted out, here — two leagues from Caldeirão. . . ."

The men were armed and surrounded me. Silently they examined the contents of my knapsack and asked to see my documents. Naked and unarmed, I could only put my faith in the power of trust and non-violence. I answered their questions, explained how I live and how I accidentally arrived at their encampment, merely looking for the chapel of Caldeirão. We were standing a few meters from the fire. All continued to look at me fixedly and in a silence full of distrust and contempt.

The man who did most of the talking and was, it seemed, their chief, though he said he wasn't, said suddenly, "See, it's three years we've been living like this, looking for a piece of land. Many people have come during these years seeking to sew disunity among us, to make us disintegrate as a group. But we're still here, because we are all one family. To survive, it's necessary for us to be distrustful. And now a fellow like you comes along wanting only to pray and to live among the poor! I never saw the like. But let's move to the fire. You can count on us."

We went to the fire and I took my place on a log. Now the conversation was more friendly, the ice had been broken and was melting before this human warmth we were creating.

A woman, certainly a mother as she had the heart of a mother, asked if I had eaten today. On hearing that I hadn't, her husband, the leader, asked her to prepare a plate for me. It soon arrived — two fried eggs, and was handed to me with a smile that illumined the night.

We talked until late. They shared some of their story with me, about not having land to plant, about their struggle and humiliations, about the temptation to become disheartened and give up. . .

It was midnight when we finally lay down to sleep. I was given an abandoned hut near the encampment.

How these people have suffered. Their distrust of strangers, a necessary tactic, shows how deeply wounded they are. The road ahead for them is long and arduous.

Next morning, following their directions, I arrived at Caldeirão. The entrance to the top of the ridge gave a fine view but there still remained an hour's climb in which I did not meet anyone. From this entrance up to the chapel all is part of Caldeirão. Thousands and thousands of hectares.

The land is dry and abandoned now. Some cotton plants in the midst of the brush and thorns, dressed in pretty white hoods, gave evidence that these lands were once cultivated. The dugouts were destroyed along with the sugar mill, the sheds where corn and manioc were ground and everything that the spirit of love and solidarity had built over the years.

The promised land had become a land of desolation.

Only the chapel remained but it was closed, locked, forbidden. Nobody now climbs its steps to pray. The cross on high challenges time, but for how long!

Only one family lives here, poor, isolated in this immense, abandoned land. They are in charge of the padre's cattle, and he's the owner here.

The key to the chapel is in the hands of the padre's cousin. He lives two leagues from Caldeirão. I went there to see if I could possibly pray in the chapel.

He gave me the same chilly reception I had received at the encampment the night before, the same distrust. Is everybody who shows an interest in Caldeirão suspect?

"What group do you belong to? Are you perhaps scouting for an invasion of this land? Where are your documents? What are you going to do in the chapel?"

Here too, the wound is festering. An abyss. . .Will there ever be a reconciliation? Will trust ever be restored?

Returning to Juazeiro do Norte, I reflected long over these two days and these striking encounters. I had gone merely to know Caldeirão and its chapel but I ended up running headlong into the two opposing forces of this terrible history.

It's as if history had presented here the opportunity to remedy the past, to help create the Kingdom of God; but what remains of the experiment is bitterness, distrust, even hatred in so many hearts.

I go everywhere unarmed and this is what gives me the permission to enter. To have nothing — only trust in the sweet Trinity. . .

When the flowers of the sertão and of the heart bloom. . .

Caldeirão,
February, 1992

The desolate lands of Caldeirão are now green. They only needed a bit of rain! The sertão flourishes once more, life surges back, it is nature's Easter. . . .

The river is flowing and the fresh, pure water is a blessing after my long, hot journey. I arrived Sunday at noon.

I passed the spot where once stood the house of the holy man, Zé Lourenço. Only the foundation of rocks from the river and some burnt timbers, burrowed through by termites remain. And there stands the chapel with its cross aloft and nearby the stone house of Oswaldo, Flora and their children.

Descending the hillside, still some distance from the chapel and the house, I hear dogs barking. Now I see the silhouette of Oswaldo on his porch. He waves to me in recognition, a gesture of welcome, and I feel encouraged. It seems the chill of my first visit has vanished.

In fact, this time I have a wonderful welcome: "You've come!" called out Oswaldo, inviting me in. Nor was it necessary this time to ask for the key to the chapel. Oswaldo himself went to fetch it and unlocked the door. Caldeirão chapel!

I took off my hat and knelt. In the silence I could hear the life of that long ago community of over one thousand families. I could hear the laughter of the children, the conversations of the women, the hoes of the men digging in their fields. . . . I heard the donkeys carry their burdens of cane to the mill, the fire crackling in the stone furnace of the flour mill, the red hot iron, forged and beaten into the shapes of hoes and sickles. I heard the washerwomen wringing out clothes on the great rock in the river, the beans boiling in their clay pots over wood fires. . . . I heard the bell peal and the steps of worshippers ascending the stairs to the chapel. The chapel is filled with people, people of the sertão, laboring people, religious people. A voice breaks the silence singing a benediction and a thousand voices pick up the refrain.

And then in the silence, I hear the destruction, the weapons speaking more loudly than the dream of peace. . .the fire reducing it all to ashes, the hatred destroying the works and dreams of all these years of love.

I let it all echo and reecho in me, all these songs as well as the shouting, the pain, the destruction. I offered it all up rising like incense here in this chapel miraculously saved — offered it all up to the Father of mercy. Offered it all up here in this chapel where the very stones learned — and today perpetuate — the prayer of the people of Caldeirão, the people of the sertão.

But Oswaldo, kneeling beside me, murmured at last, "Let's go home. Night is falling and Flora has prepared soup. But you need to wash off the journey — let's take a bath in the river."

Our swim was both communion and complicity. We jumped into the river's own "Caldeirão" a huge natural cauldron that the water carved out of rock, eight meters deep, Oswaldo told me, not without a certain pride. It was this rock depression that gave the region its name.

At supper Oswaldo said he would be planting rice tomorrow, taking advantage of the rain. We made out then that I would leave for Nova Olinda, the municipal seat, only in the afternoon it being just three leagues away. That would leave the morning for us to plant rice together.

After supper we sat on the porch playing with the children. The couple shared their joy at living in this place as well as the pain of isolation.

Later they prepared a bed for me in their living room. "Today you sleep in our house," said Oswaldo.

We got up early as is the custom in planting time. Working with the hoe wasn't half bad! Digging the stony soil, seeding the grains, tamping down the holes. . . .

Resting after lunch I sensed that Oswaldo would like me to stay longer. He hadn't explicitly asked this but the invitation was left open. "If you wish, the house is yours," he had said during lunch. And when he picked up his hoe again I did likewise and together, accomplices without words, we went to plant rice.

Returning in the evening, I said, "My help was little. You did three times as much as I did."

"Ah," he said, "but your presence was my joy. Let's take a swim in the river before supper."

On the way to the river, he murmured shyly, "If you think it's OK, perhaps we could pray the rosary in the chapel tonight. Today it's a year since my mom died. I would like to have a mass read but it's so far. . .And I'm out of money for this month."

Mystery of God. . .What are we, except useless servants? The Trinity awaits from us our availability, our trust, even to the extent of blind trust. The Trinity prepares the way — her tenderness extends to all men and women in their life's journey. It is not necessary to "do" much — just trust, abandon oneself, allow God to act. . . .

When we arrived at the house there was an air of festival. Over a wood fire a chicken was roasting. I was covered with shame — wanted to say it wasn't necessary — the daily rice and beans would do. The padre, the owner of Caldeirão who ought to be bringing the family groceries once a month doesn't do even this much. Vegetables and fruit, meat and coffee — all these are lacking.

But when Flora looked up, her eyes shining, her smile lit up the darkness. All I could do was thank her and compliment her. This night was special.

We prayed the rosary in the chapel, with the children. Oswaldo, this man of few words, was overcome with emotion and we all felt it. We meditated on the mysteries of the Trinity, the invitation to be seated at the table of love and communion, of which his mother was already partaking.

Our farewell on Tuesday morning was not easy. I promised to return. Caldeirão fascinates me and attracts me, and the new-found friendship with Oswaldo, Flora and their children bids me fulfill that promise.

Pilgrim of encounter with the Trinity

"As soon as Abraham saw them he ran out to meet them. . ."
(Gen 18: 2)

A pilgrim lives for meetings. They are gifts from the Father to enrich the journey, the manna of each day, "the bread that delighted every palate" (Wis 16: 20), more sweet to the heart than honey to the tongue.

These encounters have all the colors of humanity's rainbow. They offer a symphony of faces, of looks, of smiles from Amandina, "the prettiest girl of Brazil," to an aged couple I met in France "she, so sweet," and "he, so good." Their name is multitude, a procession of "all the nations, tribes, peoples, and tongues" (Apoc 7: 9) the anticipation of full communion in the kingdom of our heavenly Father.

In each such encounter that the pilgrim experiences is something of the mystery of God. God shares himself in such encounters when they are authentic and genuine meetings.

Encounter is gift and welcome; it is sharing and communion. It becomes thus a parable of the mystery of the most sweet Trinity, an invitation to be seated at the table of the supreme Encounter with the three travellers that Abraham met and welcomed.

José of Garanhuns

Pernambuco,
June, 1992

I've been walking from Garanhuns to here, Rio Formoso. What a lovely week! After walking on the ancient train tracks running from Garanhuns to São Benedito, I left the rail line for a sandy path of great natural beauty, far from the asphalt. My only company was a river running through this valley. Walking through such places is pure grace. Alone with mother nature, one lets her take charge of the journey. Everything sings, everything praises! What harmony is ours to experience!!

After São Benedito, the train tracks reappear. Travelling becomes more difficult, one's feet get sore. But the joy of the journey and the mysteries of one's encounters make the pain seem trivial.

One such encounter, revealing to the pilgrim the always new face of the most sweet Trinity, happened on the first day of this lovely week.

I had left Garanhuns a mere two hours earlier. At this altitude the early morning is very cold. Fog and drizzle were my companions. But even so joy sang in my heart as I followed this narrow, sandy trail. From far off I saw a little chapel some two hundred meters from the trail — an isolated chapel, a few steps leading up to it. It seemed a perfect place for me to pause, to read a little in the Scriptures, to pray in union with all who come here to pray.

I sat on the steps a moment to rest. It was a little chapel, made of clay and wattles, painted white with blue doors and windows. Humble, unpretentious, suited to its rural setting. Multitudes of little birds flying in and out told me that this place was abandoned by human beings but inhabited by them. There was beauty in this rhythmic dance of in and out, a harmony in this "movimento perpetuo" which surely caused our heavenly Father to smile as he watched. This little chapel was still his house, and even if people no longer came here to pray, the dance and the song of the birds would rise in praise like incense.

The wind and fog made me shiver. I had come from deep in the sertão where the word "cold" has a different meaning and was wearing just a short-sleeved shirt. I hadn't expected to be journeying through these lands, through this "Pernambucan Switzerland."

The little icon of the most tender Trinity, some wayside flowers, my bible open — suddenly the abandoned chapel was alive again. It was making welcome a little pilgrim who had come to meditate and was now joining his praises to those of the birds, of the fog and of the wind.

I was reading the gospel when a man appeared. I recognized him. Our paths had crossed some fifteen minutes earlier and we had wished each other good day. He had returned now carrying a hoe. I smiled and said, "On your way back then?"

"Yes. I'm going to plant manioc. I just went for a hoe. You're travelling? You came from Garanhuns?"

"Yes, I am. Here's a nice spot for a little rest. This little chapel. . .?"

"It used to belong to the Assembly of God, but they left. Now it belongs to the birds."

We talked for some time — a friendly exchange, dissipating the morning cold. Shouldering his hoe once more he said, "Let's go."

I usually accept such invitations. He was old and I had full confidence in him. We followed a little path through the fields. Five hundred meters further on we arrived at his house, a humble affair all surrounded by fields. He showed me where he was planning to plant manioc. His wife was already working there.

We had coffee and a tasty mango. Something about this man surprised me. A few pointed questions of his plus some comments as well as his trust and his serenity showed that he understood very well the kind of life I had undertaken to live. How could he know? My daily routine did not seem at all strange to him. Our conversation consisted of few words but even so we felt a wonderful communion. The warmth of his home and of this encounter filled my heart with joy. What mystery of God is in these meetings!

But it was time to head to the field. In our new-found trust and friendship he proposed quite simply that I help him plant manioc.

"Good!" I said. And so we spent the morning working side by side and conversing.

Then he told me this story. He was part of a group of migrants travelling six months here, six months there. He had been to innumnerable places in Brazil. He continued,

"We were shunted from here to there, always with the illusory hope of finding permanent employment somewhere, something human. All we were was just a labor force, two hands, a machine. When I worked without complaint, I was considered OK. But if I opened my mouth about some injustice, then I was fired.

We were lodged in these workers' barracks — you know what it's like: sometimes more than twenty in one room! And we had to endure this month after month. I don't think it ever occurred to the boss that we might expect something better. But, accept it or get kicked out. We had no other option, no. . . .

I never felt treated like a human being. We had no right to have feelings, to like a place, to stay put. . . ."

After lunch we continued our talk. When I said it was time for me to resume my journey he said, "The sun is already going down. Go tomorrow. Stay with us for the night."

That evening he told me more. After having scrimped and saved for five years he returned to the land of his birth here in Garanhuns. He rented at first while building this house on his little farm. He married Zanira from Garanhuns and had come here to live a few months earlier. "The land is good," he said, "and one can make a go of it even with very few acres."

José's and Zanira's house breathed gentleness and serenity, the fruit of the life they live.

When I said good-bye next morning early, they gave me a scarf against the cold and a blessing to protect me on my travels.

Old peddlers

Pernambuco,
January, 1992

I met José on a path, a deserted trail far from everywhere. He was waiting for me with two sacks brim full. When he saw me approaching he became excited: "Hey, old friend! How good to be together on this dangerous road. See that burned woods? The police killed a peddler right there last week. Killed him and then burned his body. There's lots of patches of burnt woods hereabouts, you understand! All along the whole road. . . . That's the way it is here. Come closer."

I came up to him and he said in a low voice, "It's because there's lots of marijuana here — many people plant it. It's the region for it, you understand? Yes, yes, much violence here. It's the law of silence you know. But for guys like us it's OK. Only don't get caught on the road. The police don't try to find out if you're mixed up in the drug trade or not. They just kill and burn."

Up to that moment I hadn't said a single word. He talked and talked. . . . From his manner of talking, from his vocabulary and by the subjects he broached it wasn't hard to guess that he had been a peddler. But the sacks, one full of bones from a slaughter house, the other full of fruits and vegetables from the weekend market, told me that this was no longer the case. He really ought to have a corner somewhere to ply his trade. It was difficult doing alone, he ought to have a companion, perhaps another peddler.

Though I don't like to be stopped on such dangerous roads as these, (he described them aptly) I was happy to meet him. Such encounters are gratuitously given us on our pilgrimage. We don't choose the place, we don't choose the hour. Our business is to welcome the meeting. . . . There is always some mystery of God to be experienced on each such occasion.

I prepared myself for a long wait while hoping for a lift in a passing vehicle as that was obviously what he was waiting for. It would most likely be a long wait.

He resumed his monologue, "My name is José. I've been all over this Brazil! And I tell you, buddy, what I've been through is no joke. You know that hospice in Campo Grande? Ask anybody there who José is, José from the sertão. They all know me. But I've calmed down a lot. My girlfriend had become pregnant, you know. We've been travelling together for years. We raised three children in our time as peddlers. Three boys. That wasn't child's play, no way! But this baby was a girl. That was no life for a little girl. We had to give up peddling. We found a little place alongside Old Chico, you know, the São Francisco River. The baby is ten months now. Pretty as all get-out — you'll see."

"So now, to eke out a living, I go to markets. I'm coming from Paulo Afonso right now. I sell my wares in Petrolandia, Floresta. . . . It's legal, you know. And now everybody knows me already. See these bones? A fellow kept them for me, I swear it. When he saw me he said, 'Aha! You've come! I've kept these bones just for you!' You see — it's above board, not so?"

Just then a truck approached. José stood practically in the middle of the road, frantically waving his hand. The Mercedes didn't slow down.

"It's always that way — they're all the same. But Chico's got to be passing by here soon. He's coming back from Paulo Afonso in a little while. He's going to take us to our little ranch in his Ford 4000. You're going to like it. And with these bones I'm going to cook us up a first-rate soup! Strong like you won't believe. You're going to see how I can cook.

You know, guy, this is great meeting you here like this. I wasn't feeling safe alone. A D-20 gave me a ride just outside Paulo Afonso but the fellow let me off here. It's not good being here alone, no. . . ."

I looked at the burnt patch of woods. It was hard to tell how much of José's story was true. I've heard stories like this often. Too often for them to be mere legends or even plain lies. I felt the cold tingle in my spine but the presence of José was comforting and reassuring.

Many trucks passed by. None of them, it seems, was the hoped-for Chico, the same Chico that seems to be on the lips so many peddlers. It's the "Chico" of hope. . . .

José told me stories of his adventures on the roads of Brazil, down the many years of his wandering. Peddlers have lots of stories — stories which never seem to find an ending. . . .

The sun began to go down. After four hours of waiting for "Chico" he arrived — arrived and stopped. But his truck wasn't the one expected. Nor had he come from Paulo Afonso but from Delmiro Gouvéia. And he wasn't from Pernambuco either but from Paraiba. And furthermore the driver's name was Pedro. As we jumped up on top of the loaded truck, José yelled, "This Chico — I've known him for years. He always gives me a ride. Good guy. Let's go, Chico!!!"

And Pedro took off. No — Chico!

Twenty kilometers further on he dropped us off on the shore of the São Francisco River. It was a stony spot, no grass, a few trees, a dry, deserted place. Was this place inhabited — or even habitable? I saw no house, just stones. But José didn't lose his enthusiasm and with great animation he exclaimed, "Well now, here's our little ranch! Terrific, not so?"

I looked in vain for "the little ranch." We crossed the road and followed a path through the stones — and there between two tall rocks was a canvas tent, torn and patched, enough to provide a little shade but that's all.

José called out. Someone answered and presently a woman appeared with a child in her arms. She had a sweet face, a timid voice. She glanced at me furtively. She was very brown and had long hair. Her skirt was ample and brightly colored and she wore a white blouse. Really, she was a flower in this stony desert. José took his daughter in his arms and exclaimed, "Just look! This is my little girl. The prettiest in all Brazil!"

His wife smiled. The little girl was delighted to see her father. José put her in my arms and I asked the mother what her name was. But it was José who answered: "Amandina. Pretty, not so? It was Janaina who gave it to her."

Amandina and Janaina. Pretty names yes, for two lovely ladies. Janaina is exactly the right name for so lovely and sweet a woman. She must be from Bahia! Janaina, José and Amandina. . . , an isolated family in a deserted place. . . .

I stopped two days with these veteran peddlers. José never lost his liveliness — perhaps it was second nature. Janaina was as sweet and tender as her name suggests. And Amandina, the pure and innocent new-born!

But even so I felt afflicted. I felt in me a muffled cry, an inaudible groan — a suffering without a name, a misery on which no one had pity. . . .

To begin with, there was this material destitution — no house, no hut, no shelter. Only this piece of torn canvas rigged up to give the illusion of a shelter. We slept outside this "tent" on the flattest rocks we could find. If it rained there would be no place to run. Under the hot sun of midday there would be no shade.

For the first time in my life I felt nauseous over a meal: it was the famous soup of bones and marrow that José had prepared with so much care and enthusiasm. While eating this "broth" I recalled what folks salvaged from garbage dumps in São Paulo, or Lima; of vegetable soups made of leftovers after market days in Recife; of dishes with strange ingredients in the Andes or from the jungle of Amazonia. They all seemed at this moment to be more appetizing than this soup made of water, bones and marrow.

Actually, their material destitution seemed of little concern to José and Janaina. Have they learned to sublimate this kind of thing or have they perhaps forgotten to some degree their human dignity? I doubt they chose this style of living freely. Did they have any alternatives, any other option?

But there is an even greater deprivation in the secret depths of their hearts — a loss that I encounter often in these one-time peddlers who at some point give up peddling.

They dream, and they dream, and at last they lose even the dream. They await something — they leave behind everything in search of some illusory goal that seems always near but escapes them. They sacrifice their lives in the name of a liberty that traps them in the prison of their fantasy.

They try so hard — and they always lose. They lose themselves in the cross-currents of philosophies, of theosophies, of strange religions, of mystic chimeras coming from afar, and even from ancient times. They have no foundation on which to build. They say they believe in everything, from reincarnation to resurrection, from God as person to God as energy, from Brahma to Mohammed, and they end up believing in nothing. They lack a faith specific enough for their becoming rooted, a faith on which to construct a history, their own personal story.

And then one day they stop, disillusioned, deceived, bitter at not having found what they expected of society, what they dreamed of, what they sought. They stop tired, exhausted.

Out of their past they still have stories to tell in the nights and in the days that are left of their lives. But they are not the stories of their personal life experience. Their personal past remains empty. Something is lacking, a unifying thread, a light, a presence. . . .

For the future there may remain some scrap of their dream that they have not relinquished even though they know they will never realize it. "Chico" will arrive one day with his winged truck!

They live in a present they didn't choose, in a world they didn't make and in which they are lost. They are far from home, banished, from another time, another space. They are strangers on the earth, living in permanent exile, shipwrecked with their disillusioned dreams.

Janaina and José.

From their exclusion, their exile, their shipwreck on the ocean of time, perhaps they have a message for us. Perhaps their very being is a sign, an alarm that we face an imminent peril, and that peril is upon us!

Perhaps they should remind us that a man and a woman are more than just two beings subjected to the determinations of time and place. Perhaps they have a message for all of us who are conformed to the mores of the world and society, who manage to become falling stars or achieve ephemeral glories in this world. . . .

Should they maybe raise some doubts in us about our accepted certitudes, adopted with so little thought. . . , like "that's the way it should be," or "that's the way the world is." "We'll always have war," we say; "there'll always be hunger. You'll never get rid of injustice; you'll always have rich and poor, exploiters and exploited. Ours is the best of all possible worlds. . . ."

A Sunday in Massapé

In the sertão,
September, 1994

It was almost necessary for me to get lost in order to arrive at this place. Massapé is a little small-holders' community of fewer than thirty houses arranged in a square around a tiny church. There are no streets, just this square. Lost in the sertão, it's some dozen leagues from the municipal seat, and three leagues from another community. Between them is desert, endless desert with scorched earth, dried brush — a waterless, lifeless desert burning under an unfeeling sun. For years it has not experienced the caressing shade of even one cloud.

I arrived here last night and I don't know how I managed it. In the last community I passed through, four leagues back, some people talked me into taking a short-cut to my destination Lagoa Seca. I trusted their advice — I trusted them and arrived instead in Massapé, five leagues from Lagoa Seca!!!

But what a blessing. . . . How our Father prepares things for us. . . .

I was welcomed at once by a family where the dad wanted to know all about the bible. So many questions. Under a star-studded sky, for it was new moon, a little crowd had gathered in front of this family's house. And so we talked at length in the peace and tranquillity of this night until Saturday came to an end and it was Sunday.

Before lying down to sleep we prayed together in the family's prayer corner dedicated to St. Thérèse of the Child Jesus. We made a prayer of self abandonment and trust, just as Thérèse would have done.

Today is Sunday, the Lord's day. I normally don't travel on Sunday. I liked to distinguish it from the other days of the week.

In the morning I visited all the houses to pray with the families. Always there was a sick grandpa, a child with a cough, something to justify requesting me to visit. It was important that I enter each house, listen to the family, drink an espresso and pray with them in their oratory asking for a blessing on the house, the family, their lives. . . .

In the afternoon we opened the little church, locked for I don't know how long. A thick layer of dust lay everywhere. The smell of mould filled the air. With the help of the young folks we organized a work bee — brooms, buckets of water, lots of energy. The spirit of fun took charge and chased the dirt. Young fellows fixed benches, girls looked for flowers and washed and starched the altar linens. Our rejuvenated little church was lovely and radiant as it welcomed us for that night's celebration.

On this Sunday night candles on the altar and little lamps on the walls brightened what had lain abandoned all these years. In the center of the square and of the community the church spread its joy over every house in a festival of transfiguration.

So blessed a Sunday. . . . The night now envelopes everything. The church and the houses are in repose.

I didn't know how I was going to spend this Sunday far from every-thing, lost in the desert. . . . But it's enough to trust — just to trust. God prepares everything. It wasn't mere chance, nor the fact that I had wandered about lost in that desert that brought me here. It was because here was the place for me to spend that Sunday, that day of the Lord.

"God then blessed and sanctified the seventh day and set it apart as a special day because by that day he had completed his creation and stopped working."

(Gen 2: 3)

"Stay with Jesus" — the lost encounter

Sergipe,
May, 1993

Today was the right day for travelling. "It's near," they said when I left the last village. But "near" was more than six leagues. Had I known I might not have gone. Added to the four leagues I had already walked in the morning, my injured foot would surely have counselled me not to go.

Altogether that made ten leagues — ten leagues in this desert area of Sergipe with a house only at rare intervals. Ten leagues on these dusty roads of clay and having to cross two streams without bridges! Ten leagues under this burning sun, no cloud to give me shade, and of course no trees in this barren sertão.

From afar I saw the city. Only one and a half leagues more. But the church tower, tall and white, spurred me on to complete the journey. A voice was telling me, "Go! Someone is expecting you!"

Tired and sweaty, thirsty and hungry and with my injured foot bleeding all along the way, I finally arrived in the town square longing for a shower. As is my custom, I headed first for the church.

What luck! It was open at this hour. I entered and knelt in silence in front of the one who was expecting me. I closed my eyes. Jesus was there. I abandoned myself to the mystery represented by the vigil light. The presence that had accompanied me the whole day was awaiting me here. I hummed the refrain that had been going through my mind the whole long day, just three words. Three words set to a few sweet, light notes: "Jesus, beloved Lord; Jesus, beloved Lord."

Suddenly six people entered the church to pray. From their songs I recognized them as charismatics. The church was now a bit noisy and I sought the sweet Trinity in interior silence.

When the group finished their prayer, two of the women approached me, wanting to talk. How lovely! Approaching one another is, after all, a gift from God.

But they had only questions. . . . So many questions! "From where do you come? Where are you going? Have you been travelling long? How do you eat, where do you sleep? Why is your bible open? Why the icon? What does it all mean?" I tried to respond patiently to each question, even though they came pell-mell.

Once the women had found out — I think! — what they wanted to know, including that the day's march had been long, that I was weary to exhaustion, that my foot hurt, and that my stomach was empty, they suddenly said, "Well we're going now. Jesus loves you. Stay here with Jesus!"

My heart leaped with joy! To stay here with Jesus! He was so present with me today. Without his presence and that of the Father, without the breath of the Divine Spirit, I never would have made it here. How good of these ladies to let me stay here with Jesus and not to have taken me along to be exclusively with them.

But I was still hungry and thirsty, sweaty and tired! My foot was still bleeding and I desperately wanted a bath. . . .

When I left the church, night had already fallen. I asked for water at a small bar to satisfy my thirst. At a gas station on the outskirts of town I found a greasy tap where I could wash my face and arms and somewhat refresh myself. The health station is shut and tomorrow is Sunday. My injured foot will have to wait. . . .

I returned to the square in front of the church. The church was now closed. I sat down on a bench under a ferny tree and let the cool air of the evening sweep over me. I felt so happy and free!

The reason was simple: Jesus was with me. . . .

Walking with a pilgrim people

"Our people like pilgrimages."
(Pueblo, 232)

God's people are a pilgrim people from all eternity and forever and ever. From Abraham to John the Baptist, men and women have sought out sanctuaries in which to celebrate their faith, or go to seek God in deserted places.

Jesus too pilgrimaged with his people. Even as a new-born he was brought in faith by Mary and Joseph to the temple. And in faith he accompanied them to Jerusalem at the age of twelve to celebrate the Passover. Taking on in faith his divine Sonship, he made the pilgrimage to Mt. Sion, to the holy city, to the sanctuary of sanctuaries.

The Christian church is a pilgrim church. The author of the letter to the Hebrews affirms this:

> *"We are all foreigners and refugees, pilgrims on this earth; we do not have here a permanent abode but we are on the search for the home that is to come."*
>
> *(Heb 11: 13 and 14)*

Vatican Council II also presents us as a pilgrim church
(Lumen Gentium, 128-139)

In our own day the people of God continue this ancient pilgrimage tradition. In pilgrimaging they not only celebrate their faith but seek an encounter with their God. Journeying in faith they construct the city that is to come, the heavenly Jerusalem, the kingdom we eagerly await. Even when our pilgrimage is not formally such in that it isn't scheduled by a specific time and place, nonetheless we rejoice to live among God's people as perpetual pilgrims. With the psalmist we sing,

> *"I rejoiced when they said, 'Let us go up to the house of the Lord.'*
> *And now we are here, standing inside the gates of Jerusalem."*
>
> *(Ps 122: 1 and 2)*

Canindé of St. Francis of the Stigmata, Canindé of the scourged sertão

Canindé,
September, 1994

Two days ago I arrived here at Canindé in the state of Ceará, this famous shrine of St. Francis of the Stigmata, popular pilgrimage destination for the people of the sertão.

I travelled for two weeks through the recesses of Ceará's sertão to get here. The "winter," that is, the rainy season, had been good everywhere and the bean harvest, the corn harvest, as well as all sorts of pumpkins and melons brought general rejoicing here where hunger had reigned for three years. Not all the dugouts had filled with water however, even now after the rains.

But now the hot sun of the dry season was scorching the land. Nowhere was there a green tree nor green grass. The mandacaru and its relatives of the cactus world rule this dried landscape, burned to ash.

Daily I walked leagues and more leagues sometimes coming upon lost communities in forgotten places, but most often encountering no signs of life — no house, no barking dog, no crowing rooster. . . . Not even a bit of shade could I find to relieve my poor body, burning under the sun, nor water to slake my thirst. . . . I did see snakes along the stony trails, once a fox crossed my path and occasionally a wildcat, the dreaded hunter of the night.

The sertão, this physical and human desert, was forged to the measure of its dryness.

The people of the sertão are the color of its earth, burned and marked by suffering. They are taciturn and deep, trusting and tough. Their capacity to endure is legendary. They acquired from their dry and thirsty land the perpetual hope that a cloud might come to caress it. It's a hope that is hard to feel or to imagine, but from it gushes a faith rooted in the entrails of mother earth, in the innermost and secret recesses of their being.

It shows itself in their faith, in the prayer corners to be found in every home, in the crosses put up along the ways, in the village chapels.

And this faith shows itself especially here at St. Francis of the Stigmata in Canindé. This devotion to St. Francis who received in his body the wounds of Jesus didn't just find a home in Canindé by accident. Is not the sertão itself scourged?

Cracked earth, dried bushes, abandoned and rotting carcasses, and the drought. . .the people of the sertão have experienced in their person all the scourges of this land.

Their faith is manifest in the people. It is a transparent faith because it is true, authentic. It radiates from their very being. One can read on their faces that which is in their hearts, the faith that has its lodging there, and from which they draw life.

One sees it in a smile, a gesture of the hand, a welcoming word, their shining eyes. . . . One reads it in the sign of the cross they make before and after meals, as they leave on a journey, or pass a church. It's revealed in their lighted candles, their night prayer in their prayer corner, their vigil light burning, keeping watch during the shadows of the night. It's visible in the blessing the children of the sertão ask from their parents, godparents or relatives:

"A blessing, mother!"
"God bless you."
"A blessing god-mother!"
"May God keep you happy!"
"A blessing, grandpa!"
"May God give you health."
"A blessing, uncle!"
"May God grant you peace."

That is the faith of the sertão's people, a faith that finds here in Canindé its most privileged place of expression.

It's the faith that moves mountains, that brings the pilgrims here annually in multitudes either walking over these dry rock-strewn trails or making the difficult journey loaded in trucks — here to Canindé, to St. Francis of the Stigmata.

We have much to learn from the faith of these folk of the sertão. . . .

A pilgrim in the church's springtime. . .

Through the force of the gospel, the Holy Spirit rejuvenates the Church, continually renewing it and bringing it to union with her spouse.

(Lumen Gentium, 4)

"The Spirit and the Bride say, 'Come, Lord Jesus.' "

(Rev 21: 17)

By way of introduction. . .

One of the graces given to a pilgrim is that of being a witness. The roads of the world lead one along an infinity of paths and byways where one can contemplate all the colors of humanity. Though one's steps lead to a sharing in people's suffering, yet one's eyes never tire of marvelling at the beauty revealed everywhere, in every situation, with every person — beauty that suddenly reveals itself even in the green hell of the cane lands.

At the end of this second millenium the Holy Spirit blows over the Church so sweetly, so ardently that it is bringing men and women of faith to a genuine living of the gospel, the good news of Jesus Christ, seeking to build the Kingdom of the Father today, here on earth, for all the human family. These men and women, "from every tribe, tongue, people, and nation" (Apoc 5: 9) are renewing the Church, the temple of the Spirit. They are creating a springtime in the Church.

The pilgrim is witness to this. Wherever he travels, he finds the seeds of faith germinating, buds bursting open, fragrant blossoms, flowering trees, fields garlanded for a festival. The signs are simple and humble as are all signs of the Kingdom, fragile as a flower, delicate as a fragrance.

Pilgrimaging through these springtimes I had many experiences that gave witness to such hopes. I choose three as representative of their general tenor.

They will remain anonymous, imprecisely located in time and space so as not unduly to exalt either persons or situations, but illustrating how multitudes of men and women are conducting their lives according to the gospel.

"Each of us in our humble place is Church," wrote St. Augustine. I select a parish from the interior, a fraternity in a slum, and another in the sertão: varied contexts, therefore, diverse protagonists, but it's the same breath animating all three, the breath that animates the Church.

> *"There are different kinds of gifts but the same Spirit gives them. There are different ways of serving but the same Lord is served."*
>
> *(1 Cor 12: 4-5)*

The desert Fathers speak of "<u>uncreated</u> Light" the light that enveloped Jesus on the Mount of the Transfiguration, which is also the Light of the Resurrection. I believe that everywhere where the Church is experiencing a springtime this light is to be found shining. Every fragrance of these hopes has the power of Transfiguration, each flower of these springtimes is a sign of the Resurrection.

And, if the eyes of our heart were able to contemplate such light, then, in an instant, the five continents would light up with thousands upon thousands of little sparkling flames. This is the great hope of the Church, of humanity.

May these lines be dedicated to all the servants of God in all the earth who seek to obey the breath of the Divine Spirit (1 Sam 15: 21-22) creating a new springtime of the Church.

These men and women fulfill the hope of the Church as expressed in Vatican Council II, the first fruits of this springtime:

> *"The pilgrim Church carries the stamp of the present century; she lives amid creatures who groan in the act of giving birth and who wait the revelation of the children of God."*
>
> *(Lumen Gentium, 130)*

I The parish — basic church community

In the sertão,
February, 1992

I find myself in one of these lost municipalities of the sertão, at "the end of the world" as folks here call it. And it is. . . .

To arrive here I had to cross the same river twice. Bridges and asphalt are unknown in these parts. In the sertão's winter, the rainy season, this municipality is totally cut off, isolated. . . . One can only get here by foot. And even so I had to cross that river with water up to my neck.

The end of the world! "It's near here," they told me about mid-afternoon, "only a league away."

But it was night before I got there, all tired out by the day's travel of seven or eight leagues. It's Holy Thursday and on the way I kept thinking that there might be a service in the church. I offered up to the Father my desire to celebrate on this day.

On arriving, I noticed immediately that there were lights in the church. That awakened an ardent hope. In the square in front of the church a large crowd was watching a soap opera on a public TV set. That's common in these isolated municipalities of the sertão. But, despite its lights, the church seemed to be closed. However I did find a side door to be ajar.

I entered, a bit furtively. Nobody about. I called out — nobody answered. But the eucharistic vigil light shone. He was there, awaiting me. I knelt and adored. I read the thirteenth chapter of John, the washing of the feet. The stillness inside the church matched the silence of the street and the stillness of my heart. I lost all notion of time. It seemed like only a moment, like a ray of time, these intimate hours with Christ. I remembered the words of a Russian pilgrim:

"Walking through the countryside for days, even for weeks, unable to receive the body and blood of Christ, the repetition of Jesus' name brought me into intimate communion with the Lord just as if I had been receiving communion."

The night was already advanced when an elderly man came to the door. He saw me and with great simplicity he said, "Ah, you are praying, stay as you are. I'll come back in half an hour to close the church."

And he went out leaving me to the peace of the church. I was overjoyed to be able to continue praying in this silence. At nine o'clock he returned to lock up.

"Well," he said, "you must be a man of God, walking like that, eh? And a good walker. . . ! I suppose you have no place to sleep, but you know, in the other square is a little hotel. If you talk to the owner — her name is Rosa — everybody knows Dona Rosa — she will make you welcome. You probably don't have any money but Rosa is a good person, she won't turn you away."

I have never asked for a room in a hotel for which I couldn't pay, but it seemed to me this man had been sent to me by God himself. . . . I went to find Rosa. Her little "hotel" was simply her house with a couple of rooms for guests. It appears she was known far and wide for her goodness — but also for her corpulence! Dona Rosa was a "big mama" as people call a woman whose heart is ready to adopt all humanity as her children. She promised me a hammock for the night, let me take a shower and fed me a copious supper. She even fried me some eggs because the meat had all been eaten. A mother's heart indeed. . . .

Seated on her porch I reflected on the mystery of the Trinity. I had arrived here a few hours earlier tired after the long journey, the river in flood, this town always "near" but never showing up. But the Trinity was expecting me: the open church, lit for I don't know what; this time of contemplative prayer, the sacristan like an angel, pointing me here; the owner of this hotel welcoming me as a mother welcomes a son. . . . How mysterious are God's ways!

Suddenly a young man, about age thirty, appeared. He wore a cap of black leather and wore his hair at medium length. He asked me where I was from, why I was praying in church, what I wanted. . . . I thought maybe he was from the police, such things happen in situations like this. I answered quietly, as simply as possible. But when he had exhausted all his questions, he added, "I'm the padre here. Come sleep at my house."

"What? I don't understand. . . ."

"Yes, I'm the padre."

I couldn't conceal my stupefaction. I accepted his invitation, thanked Dona Rosa and excused myself. We went.

We talked until late. This padre has gifts that make one take note. The way he shares in the life of his flock is a rare and wonderful thing to see.

No priest of the diocese wanted to come to this parish, so isolated. It's a big parish in size, with communities up to twelve leagues distant from the municipal center where he was stationed.

But this new padre, recently ordained — he agreed to come here, on one condition, to live like the local people and earn his own living. And so he has his own plot where he raises beans, corn and rice. After being here only a year and a half he obtained a piece of land on which to plant a community garden. Some twenty destitute families took on the care and the work of these fields and he joined his holding to theirs without hesitation.

His house is open to all. The young people especially feel quite at home here. While we were talking there was a ceaseless coming and going. The sacristan, too, showed up with the same simplicity and humility I had noticed earlier.

With complete ease some girls came in and joined our conversation. Presently there was a sizeable group of young people sharing with us the reality of their lives in this isolated place. They talked about the community garden, about a planned pilgrimage, about church outreach to youth, about parish celebrations, both in the mother church of the parish as well as in the outlying communities. They wanted to know more about living the faith, about being true to the gospel, about satisfying the thirst for God that burned in their hearts!

The padre was mainly silent, contemplating with shining eyes this improvised and unexpected exercise in sharing. His simple manner, completely natural, showed him to be a man who knows how to create peace and harmony and to transmit these gifts to others.

Even now, I continue to be impressed with how natural it all was, and the simplicity with which the evening unfolded. To find such authentic life in a parish is to proclaim once more that the parish is "the community of Church." Here are united all manner of people, from workers in the community gardens looking for seed, to the single medical doctor of the municipality who came to schedule a meeting for the organization known as the "pastoral da criança," the church's outreach to children; and not only all classes but all ages came this evening, from a four-year-old godchild of the padre who came for his blessing, to that sacristan who carries his many years so lightly.

They showed such pleasure in just being together, in journeying with each other, in praying, in building the Kingdom. Their love is firmly rooted in the love of the Father, making of them one large family.

This was the final, indeed the only commandment of Jesus. In his farewell talk to the apostles, reported to us by John, he speaks only in these terms:

> *"And now I give you a new commandment: love one another. As I have loved you, so you must love one another. If you have love for one another, then everyone will know that you are my disciples."*
>
> *(Jn 13: 34-35)*

Just think — walking here this afternoon I offered to the Father my desire to celebrate the eucharist on this Holy Thursday. He satisfied my desire beyond all expectation. Jesus didn't only offer himself in the sacrament of the eucharist but also in the sacrament of brothers and sisters who welcome each other and in the sacrament of a parish that lives the gospel.

Such an encounter for me is light. In this town a light shines giving strength and courage to many. Joined to the many other lights of the sertão, of Brazil, of the whole world, it will disperse the shadows of gloom that hang over humanity. Such people are the hope of tomorrow, hope on the road to the Kingdom where

> *"Love and Faithfulness have met,*
> *Justice and Peace have embraced."*
>
> *(Ps 85 (84): 11)*

One doesn't need a lot to start living the gospel. . . .

II "Living Stone"
— a new heaven and a new earth

Ceará,
February, 1992

It's a privilege to be here — here in "The House by the Side of the Road." It's a house of God, and of his suffering children. It is light and hope in this slum where misery appears to rule. Misery — the only law of life, the only inheritance.

In this "House by the Side of the Road" a group of young people have lived together for the last five years. They feel called to share the life of these marginalized slum families. They have accepted this daily presence, communal and humbly simple, as their vocation. Their lives proclaim a prophetic word, give a genuine witness. They are living good news.

Here the sertão flourishes, not only the sertão of planted fields but also the sertão of hearts. For those who see only with the eyes of society, these are invisible flowers, but for those who see with the eyes of faith, they shine brilliantly.

They are the "Living Stone." Here they have a piece of land where homeless families huddled along the highway can build new houses for themselves. Nobody gives them bricks. They make them themselves, two leagues away at the river. They head for the river at four in the morning, work the clay all day, and come walking home at night. Nobody is making houses for them. They themselves are doing it — and all in work bees. All done with what means they have at hand!

Today each family has a house. A poor "house"? Yes, of course — no electricity, no running water, the floor of packed clay, the plaster a mix of earth and sand.

But dignity lives in each of these houses, with each of these families. The dad can enter his house with his head held high and say to his family, "This is our house. We are real folks."

And the mother can tell her children, and her grandchildren when they appear, with all the dignity and nobility of one recounting a story that is beautiful, a story that is holy:

"It was we ourselves who built this house, who made the bricks, mixed the concrete, raised the walls and put on the roof. We women made soup for all the families so that no one would die of hunger. That's our history. We managed it all because we stayed united and because God was with us. We prayed before each working bee, before each meal, before each meeting."

A sacred history, yes, in the primeval meaning of the word because in every history in which God is manifested, God is also revealed.

One kind of "miseria" did not move into these new homes, a misery more profound, the misery of humiliation, of sub-humanity. This they left behind with their huts of clay and wattles. It is no longer a part of them. It belongs to their past, a past to which they will never return.

I have the privilege of learning here, learning from these poor people how to be evangelized.

Here a light shines, as simple as it is marvellous. Here the prophecy of Isaiah is fulfilled:

> *"See, I am creating a new heaven and a new earth. Be glad and rejoice forever in what I create. They will build houses and will live in them. They will plant vines and eat of their fruits. They will fully enjoy the things that they have worked for!"*
>
> *(Is 65: 17-22)*

One doesn't have to be able to read and write in order to learn the gospel. One needs only to look with the eyes of faith.

III "Jesus is here,"
a community in a big city slum

São Paulo,
August, 1992

In the middle of a slum in the immense east zone of São Paulo there is a small wooden hut no different from any of its neighbors.

In the back of this house, almost hidden under a stairway, in the darkness of a windowless corner, a light shines.

This little lamp of Taizé in its red and yellow glass, casts living color in all directions. At its left is an icon of the Resurrection; to its right, one of the Trinity. A little above it is a simply carved wooden tabernacle.

Jesus is here. Here in the eucharistic presence and in the hearts of these suffering people of the slums. He is here in the open bible placed before the lamp and he is present in the words of life, of pain, and of hope that mark the men and women of this place.

Jesus is here when at four in the morning the members of this community come together in silence. It's the only hour that affords a minimum of silence. Jesus is here when the chapel fills with God's people, come to celebrate their faith.

Jesus is here with this community in the heart of this slum. His presence in this place of so much suffering has the power to transfigure lives.

In this contemplative life, in this loving presence Jesus lives.

This community has a great gift — that of welcoming the destitute, of welcoming Jesus. How many street people have they made welcome? How many single mothers, how many pregnant but homeless women, how many street children? And how many youths threatened with death or just released from prison or from the government's reform institution. The community's house is the house of all of these — these who have nowhere else to go.

When someone comes, no one asks, "Where do you come from? Where are you going? Why are you in this situation? How long do you plan to stay?"

Instead they open their arms and exclaim, "How good of you to come. Make yourself at home."

This is the house of the prodigal son's father, the house of the Kingdom of God, the house where the gospel is lived on a daily basis.

Jesus is here! Can one doubt it? And if some can't see that, let them spend a few days here. The poor point out the roads that lead to the Father. Isaiah already prophesied this in his canticles of the Suffering Servant: "I will make you a light to the nations." (Is 49: 6)

One needs only to risk beginning, to take that first step into the mud and sewage of the slum, to listen to loudspeakers blaring twenty-four hours per day, to accept the inevitable promiscuity of favelas like this where on any square meter of vacant space a little room will be put up, to continually have people calling you at the door of your hut.

It's not really necessary to do much, only allow yourself to be captivated by Marcia's smile — Marcia, suffering from AIDS, who nonetheless keeps running up and down stairs constantly to attend to her paralyzed mother. Though her mother demands continual attention, Marcia's happy smile is a constant. Or by the always open arms of Renate, little mother of "three and a half angels," she says proudly. Or by the attention of Tereza, a refugee from the drought of Ceará, sheltered — one can hardly say lodged — in a space of four square meters, fenced in by old boards. She invites us saying, "It's very small but we can sit out front! And the heart is big!!"

And there's Claudio, formerly a street boy welcomed years ago by this community. Today, still an adolescent, he lives in a little house with three other ex-street boys. He explodes with delight as he announces,

"I'm going to Morumbi!! I'm rooting for the Corinthians to win over Palmeiras and on to the championship!"

All that's needed is to pay a little attention to the kids running about on broken cement and past open sewers, where men play dominos and women chat, a baby in their arms.

Here is the people — life! Here is Jesus. In this slum and, gathering all their suffering, their joys and hopes, in this little chapel.

Here the Kingdom is happening, a new springtime, a hope for tomorrow. Here salt has not lost its flavor and the light of the gospel radiates from house to house.

Yes, it's only a little sign, and fragile! A handful of men and women of faith in the midst of a great multitude, a slum of twenty to thirty thousand inhabitants. But that's how the signs of the Kingdom are: humble, simple, innocent. Only a little yeast is needed to raise the dough, to give birth to bread.

The light shines. Yellows and reds break through the darkness illuminating icons and tabernacle.

Jesus is here.

From behind prison bars

"I was in prison, and you visited me."

(Mt 25: 36)

On arriving at any given place a pilgrim is seldom recognized as being simply that, a pilgrim. A vagabond, yes; a disturber of the peace; certainly someone on the fringes of society, someone to avoid.

Fortunately, most often, meeting people and talking to them soon dispels the distrust.

Not always, of course. Sometimes dialogue doesn't stand a chance. Distrust and fear occasionally reach such a point that the police need to intervene. They check my documents, the contents of my knapsack, accompanied at times by verbal and physical threats.

At such times the pilgrim may be put into jail. The reasons — or non-reasons! — are of no importance. A night behind the checkerboard of prison grates will then be the opportunity for a vigil, a communion with all those who are deprived of their liberty. Liberty — we only appreciate its great value when we are deprived of it.

Imprisonment in the interior of Bahia

Bahia,
July, 1990

It was late at night when I arrived at this small municipal seat in the interior of Bahia. In front of the church was a pretty little square with trees and benches. The square was completely deserted at this late hour.

I chose a bench well back, nestled between two trees, and sat down. I wrapped myself in my towel in a vain attempt to keep out the cold. The day's march had been long and tiring and I was half asleep as soon as I sat down. I expected nothing further of this day than simply a peaceful sleep. Though it was a cold night, the atmosphere seemed cozy and welcoming. I looked for nothing beyond that.

As was my custom, before sleeping I sang psalm 121, a song of trust for someone facing a night that could become dangerous:

> *"Yahweh will not let you fall;*
> *your protector is always awake.*
> *The protector of Israel never sleeps, never slumbers.*
> *The Lord will guard you;*
> *he is by your side to protect you.*
> *The sun will not hurt you during the day,*
> *nor the moon during the night.*
> *The Lord will protect you from all evil;*
> *he will keep you safe.*
> *He will protect your coming and going,*
> *now and forever."*

(Ps 121 (120): 3-8)

I ended with a thanksgiving for the day and with Charles de Foucauld's prayer of abandonment. I lay down and fell into a deep sleep.

But not for long. Someone touched my shoulder — it was a youth who said, "Would you like a shirt?"

Startled and frightened, I needed some moments to react. The young man, about twenty, had come on his bicycle and had a long-sleeved shirt in his hands. He explained:

"I saw you arrive here, tired and cold. So I thought, wouldn't it be nice if he had a blanket for the night. I went home but couldn't find a blanket, just this shirt, but it's warm. Would you like it?"

What could I do but accept. I received it as a gift from God. The young man also offered me some hot coffee that he had brought. We talked for a bit but I was overcome by sleep and stayed awake only with difficulty. Before leaving he said, "You know, at the police station they might give you a night's lodging. It's better than here in the cold. You only have to ask. They'll make you welcome."

I found this proposition a bit strange. I had never done this before. And in fact I never ask for a place to sleep no matter where! But I reflected that perhaps this youth hadn't appeared simply by chance. I resolved to test his suggestion. I went to the police station. The one officer on duty welcomed me and said, "Yes, of course, but you'll have to sleep in a cell behind bars. If that's OK with you. . . ."

Yes, of course. If I planned to sleep in a police station, that's where I would be, behind bars! I entered with the officer. The door banged shut and a chain locked me in. The noise echoed for some moments in the stillness of the night. I think the noise robbed me of the sleep that only minutes before I couldn't resist. I put the icon of the most tender Trinity on my cement bed, lit a candle, and opened the Scripture. Instead of sleep my night became a vigil, a watch between these dirty walls all scribbled, and smelling of feces. . . . I was a solitary prisoner but my vigil became a communion with all who are forgotten in prisons, for all the rejected, the excluded. . . .

Next day I had another surprise. By mid-morning I had arrived at the neighboring town, quite near actually, when a heavy downpour began. The rain didn't let up and I had to interrupt my journey. The clay road was now sticky mud. I waited in the central square under a covered shelter waiting for a car that might be going my way, a car that never appeared. But I did chat with several people. One lady, a fruit vendor, belonged to the Assembly of God. A man working in a store belonged to the same church. We talked a lot about God's Word. In such circumstances I always look for common ground, without concealing my own church roots, trying always to center the conversation on Christ as the foundation stone that unites us.

And so the whole day passed. The heavy rain continued unabated, providential considering the good experiences of the day.

But, about five in the afternoon, a military police car came at high speed and stopped right in front of me. Two men came out of the car on the run with weapons drawn, and asked for my documents. The captain, at any rate the leader, seemed very nervous. I showed my documents but he said, "We're going to the police station."

He gave me no chance to speak and so I calmly picked up my knapsack and went with them. Now, a thing like this doesn't happen every day of the week in a village like this and almost at once a large crowd gathered around the car. Entering the vehicle I experienced the full weight of public humiliation. The people's glances, their muted comments, the destructive gossip, the malicious criticisms — all terribly humiliating. Through every car window I could see eyes fixed on me, looks that were a mixture of curiosity and contempt, looks that revealed they had already judged me.

But then the man from the Assembly of God made an incredible gesture: in front of everybody he walked up to the captain and said, "May I speak?"

"Yes, of course."

"The situation with this young man is not what it appears. He is a man of God. He journeys about preaching the Word of God. There is no fault in him."

"One never knows," said the captain. "I'm going to take him in for questioning."

"OK. But I will answer for him."

I was impressed by this man's intervention. He wasn't afraid to stand up in front of everybody, even when they were loudly expressing their contempt and passing judgment. To act as he did requires courage and faith.

And so we went. But the only real problem was that the captain didn't know what to make of the documents of a foreigner. He had never seen any such before. We went to the local justice of the peace who looked at them and declared them to be in order. The captain still wanted to examine my knapsack, but all he found there was my bible, my towel and my writing materials. During this "search" the justice asked me about my activities and I answered her simply and calmly.

So then, all being in order, the captain drove me back to the town square. On the way he said, "You know, I'm a Christian, too. I belong to the Church of the Four-Square Gospel. We have a service tonight at 7:30. Would you like to come?"

I never refuse such an invitation. I accepted with delight and he added, "What will you do till then?"

I had already found out that mass would be celebrated in the church at six o'clock and I had planned to attend.

"Well then," he said, "I'll wait for you at the entrance of the church at six-thirty and you come to my house to eat. Then we'll go together to the service at my church. and later I'll arrange for you to sleep in the police station."

Thus it was spoken and thus it happened! It all got arranged so fast it made my head spin. To be taken into custody by the police, humiliated, examined and then to be invited by the same folks to eat and to go to their church service. . .

When I came out from mass the captain was waiting for me. He took me to his house where I was received with full honors. His wife had prepared a festive supper and the children stayed at the table all during the meal, giving it a real sense of celebration.

The whole family attended the service. In this village the Four-Square Gospel has only a small congregation, a sort of family affair, gathering some five or six such family groups. This gave their service an intimate dimension, a closeness and a simplicity that was beautiful to experience.

At the end of the service the captain spoke, "There is a man among us who is consecrated to God. He is a young man who devotes his entire life to the service of God's Word."

He asked me to come forward and to speak a few words. I selected from the bible the first servant song of the prophet Isaiah:

> *"He will not shout or raise his voice*
> *or make loud speeches in the street.*
> *He will not break off a bent reed*
> *nor put out a flickering lamp. . . ."*

(Is 42: 2-3)

Beginning with this text I spoke of my life among the poor, among the excluded and forgotten.

After the service the captain brought me back to the police station. Another night behind bars. But when the doors and locks clanged shut behind me I felt myself folded into the tenderness of the Trinity.

I knelt on the cell floor. The rain still echoed through the prison. This jail was much like the one I was in last night, and once again I was the only prisoner — prisoner of a single night.

But yet another surprise was in store for me. . . .

About 11 o'clock the officer appeared at my cell to say, with great embarrassment, "I know this is quite irregular, but then so is your situation. There's a girl here who wishes to speak with you. Should I let her in?"

"Yes, of course."

Moments later a young woman of about twenty-five appeared at my cell, a bible in her hands. Her long hair hung wet with the rain and she was breathing heavily, apparently having run.

After she composed herself, she smiled and said, "I'm the daughter of the lady who sells fruit in the square. She told me what happened there this afternoon, what the police did to you. I was very upset. At our church service tonight we prayed for you. When it ended I came directly here. I feared you might have been mistreated by the police. But you're OK, it seems."

I was moved by her solicitude. This was a night of communion among the churches. Jesus prayed ardently for the love that should unite all his followers.

> *"Holy Father! Keep them safe by the power of your name, so that they may be one just as you and I are one."*
>
> *(Jn 17: 11-26)*

The young lady returned home about midnight. But now sleep failed me. In my heart was a burning desire for communion. The night again became a vigil, a watch with the words of Jesus echoing through the hours:

"That they all may be one."

In jail #3

Ceará,
January, 1992

It's a cold, lugubrious night in this municipality of Ceará. It's still cloudy, following a heavy rain.

I sit down on the cold, damp cement of my cell here in jail number three straining my eyes to write. A single bulb in the corridor allows a feeble light to enter my cell. The only window is inaccessibly high; a hole in the corner serves as toilet. The floor is so wet and dirty that standing seems preferable to sitting — to say nothing of lying down! The smell of rot pervades the whole place — every wall, the floor, everything gives off the smell of rot.

The bars themselves turn oppressor. Is there any corner to give refuge?

The walls spy on every step, every gesture. The iron gratings remind me that liberty stayed outside. Being locked in arouses in me a desire to run, to fly.

On one wall a former prisoner counted the days in vertical strokes. I lost track at about fifty. On another spot was a name, Pedro Rodriguez.

Inscriptions told of anguish, of despair. I read them slowly allowing their cries to enter my heart:

João has been waiting for over fifty days for the judge to return from holidays to sign his release; fifty days, the judge still isn't back. . . . João waits. He has served all his sentence but the judge "forgot" to sign his release document and went on holidays. João is waiting. . . . He writes, "The rainy season is nearly over. If I can't plant now to take advantage of these rains, what will we eat this year?"

The raindrops on the roof now seem ominous. They speak of time passing, time that will never return, of life-giving water that will never return. I hear these echoes of João's anguish. And the judge is still in Fortaleza enjoying its beaches.

José is waiting for a visit from his girlfriend. He got five months for assault. His friend was "fooling around with my girl." Jealousy and anger — knife at the belt — blood spilled.

João couldn't read or write so he begged me to write to his girlfriend. While my pen poured out the words on paper — words of love, of regret, of despair, my heart was bleeding. A terrible wound lacerated his heart. His girlfriend still had not visited him.

This will be a night of prayer. Anyway, how could one sleep in a place like this? My candle burns in front of the icon of the Trinity and cell three became my "poustinia," my hermitage and chapel for the night. I prayed for João, for José, for Pedro Rodriguez, for all of them, with all of them. I offered up the cries that rise from these inscriptions on the walls, made with blood, made with excrement, their only writing material. I brought all this suffering to the Trinity, to the table of love, to God who alone takes on so much pain. In a place like this one can suffocate in the despair that the air itself carries.

To pray. To meditate. Here in this cell where darkness reigns by day as well as by night. Locked in, a prisoner of one night, so near to Jesus.

In the women's prison of Salvador

Salvador,
August, 1990

Back in Salvador, I participated in an encounter with the Missionaries of Christian Confraternity in order to prepare their annual all-night vigil for the feast of the Transfiguration which happens each year early in August. They have done this at various places in the city, in the base communities, in parishes, in hospitals. This year the vigil was to be held in the women's prison where several of the missionaries visit regularly.

I joined them for this Saturday to Sunday watch. Saturday morning we arrived there to make final preparations and we were able to celebrate the eucharist.

I had been in prisons before: in France where I had taught in one for a year; in São Paulo; in Santa Cruz de la Sierra. But this was my first visit to a women's prison. I sensed a big difference. The faces of these women cried out for a little tenderness, a chance to speak, to unburden themselves. I wanted to spend the whole day before the vigil would begin, praying in a room that one of the missionaries had turned into a chapel. The group agreed and so did the prison administrator. The only condition would be that I would be locked into the chapel, "for your own protection."

And so I passed the afternoon there. I wanted to fast but the women brought me orange juice, curdled milk, sweets, cheese. . . . I had no time to be alone. There were always visitors at the bars in the corridor. I listened to each one's story. They have so little opportunity to talk. Trapped behind a wall of silence they are doubly imprisoned.

Most of the women participated in the vigil. It was a night of magic.

Our text was Jesus' request of the woman at the well, "Give me to drink." (Jn 4: 7) Throughout the vigil we tried to drink from the women's personal wells, to learn from their mystic experience, the experience they had of God in the penitentiary. Sharing with them was beautiful. Profound and rich. The water they offered us became a spring of living water. . . .

At the close of the vigil, in a symbolic gesture that was meant to signify what we had experienced that night, the women gave us to drink from their own cups. We were overcome with emotion as we mixed our tears and water in an offering signifying respect and dignity.

Our goodbyes came at the dawn. One said, "My nights here are nightmares. This night was a dream." Another added, "Tonight renewed in me the flame of hope."

The heart of a child

Be humble and little in the arms of God, trusting in the Father's goodness, even to the point of being bold.

(Thérèse of the Child Jesus)

In every adult sleeps the heart of a child. Jesus came to awaken this heart. "We played the flute but you did not dance. . . ." "Unless you become like a little child. . . ." "Behold the birds and the lilies of the field!"

In our day Jesus prolongs his mission through those who have not lost this heart of a child. They are the poets and the mystics. It is the poet and the little child who dance, who dance to the sound of the flute, who exclaim in wonder at the birds and the lilies of the field.

Every child has the heart of a poet — is a poet. RUAH, the breath of God, the maternal love of the creating Father, finds in the heart of a child such liberty that it can blow there lightly and sweetly, an afternoon breeze to awaken even in blasé adults the child's heart that may lie dormant.

The following letters are stories about children. Reading between the lines you will find Édivan, Cidinha, Vitoria, Simón and their little colleagues the world over, sewing on the air their flute tones, the ones we read of in the gospel. . . .

Shall we dance?!

On the high plateau, welcomed in an Aimara home

Andean plateau,
Bolivia, February, 1990

Lake Titicaca fascinates me. It guards mystery in its secret depths. Here everything is sacred. I followed its shores for several days, far from the asphalt that circles it in a general way, not having the time to follow all of its convolutions. I looked at all of its creeks and coves, all of its beaches of fine sand, each bay where the lake's famous rushes grow.

Late one afternoon I was caught in a heavy rain. Ahead of me I saw a few houses, including one standing apart that appeared to be abandoned. I headed there for shelter. The building was indeed uninhabited, but not abandoned: some children had made of it their palace of dreams, imagining what only children can imagine as they ran about in its rooms of broken walls.

They didn't take fright on seeing me. They spoke Spanish, not always the case in these isolated communities. We were all introduced to each other and I joined in their racing and dancing, in the magical party they were creating in this palace.

What a fine encounter this sudden shower offered me! But the rain didn't let up and soon turned the floor into mud. The children and I took shelter under the only bit of roof still intact.

As it was becoming dusk the oldest asked, "Where are you going to sleep tonight?" "I don't know," I said. "We'll see if the rain stops."

"It won't stop. It's going to rain like this the whole night. You can't sleep outside. And it will be cold too. I'm going to see if mama will let you sleep in our house. That would be good! Wait here. I'll be right back."

And off he ran with his two brothers.

I had little confidence in being welcomed here, so great is the distrust between the Aimara people and the descendants of the conquistadors with whom I would naturally be identified. But I didn't let it bother me. I wrapped myself in my blanket because added to the rain an icy wind was beginning to blow. I studied the lake. The rain and the wind were transforming it, revealing another facet of its mystery. It was now the color of ash, making it look even deeper, more inscrutable. . . .

In such reflective moods I lose all sense of time. It seemed that the boy Simón returned almost immediately. All lively and happy he said, "Let's go."

He took my hand and led me to their house. When we were nearly there he said in a low voice, almost apologetically:

"You know, daddy isn't home and mama said you couldn't sleep here but there is a little shelter outside for the pigs. But there aren't any pigs in it now, OK? I penned them up down at the bottom of the back yard. I cleaned up the pig sty and put dried rushes on the ground. That way you can sleep better. Is that OK with you?"

Would that be OK. . . ? What really was OK with me that moment was that little brown hand of an Aimara Indian, descendent of an enslaved people, in my European hand, descended from the conquering colonizers. Our hands joined, his trust, his happiness — it was like a reconciliation. This was indeed good. . . . For this gift I would indeed gladly have slept in this shelter even with the pigs.

"It's better than I could have expected," I answered him. "Thanks for everything you're doing."

The rain stopped despite his forecast. The mother was on her doorstep waiting for her son and this unknown stranger. I read distrust on her face, a striking contrast to the trust of her boy. Simón must have been very insistent to wrest this much of a concession from her for this foreigner coming at nightfall. Perhaps the pig shelter was a compromise acceptable to both of them.

Despite her distrust and fear, she managed a smile and showed me the shelter, just a 2x1 meter of ground roofed over with rushes. The dry rushes on the floor welcomed me. I thanked them and just then Simón shouted, "Daddy!"

He ran to embrace his father whom nobody apparently had expected. He told his father a long story in Aimara. The father looked at me with the same distrust as had the mother. He said a few words in Aimara to his wife who hung her head and responded only in monosyllables. Simón tried to enter the conversation but with a peremptory gesture the father imposed silence. The situation had become delicate. Accepting a child's invitation can lead to such impasses. I waited for the end of the conversation, none of which I understood.

Then the father approached me and began to question me in Spanish. I answered tranquilly but didn't manage to lessen his distrust. What to do? I thought of leaving so as not to worsen an already bad situation, but I feared that Simón, animated by the purest and most praiseworthy intentions, would have to answer for it later.

Just as I was about to speak, Simón, pulling at his father's shirt sleeve and challenging his authority, exclaimed, "But dad, he has a bible!"

The dad kept looking at me but his expression began to change, to relax. He said something in Aimara to his wife and she raised her head. He asked me if I could read. On hearing that I could he asked me in a voice already less harsh, almost inviting, "Well, then, read us a passage from the life of Jesus. . . ."

The way he put his question impressed me. It was "the life of Jesus" that interested him. My meditation earlier as I had gazed over Lake Titicaca was about Jesus on the shores of the Sea of Galilee, Jesus with the fishermen, with Peter and Andrew, James and John. I guessed that this man, too, would be a fisherman. I chose the first fishing miracle in Luke and the call of the first disciples when Jesus said to Peter,

> "Head out to the deep;
> Throw out your nets for the catch."

> *(Lk 5: 1-11)*

The father listened in devout silence, deeply moved. At the end of the reading he stayed silent for some time. Then he translated it for his wife as far as I could guess, and after a pause he added something in Aimara. I didn't understand but I noted that she went into the house.

Then the father began to speak to me as to a friend. His icy distrust had been thawed by the warm heart of a child and by the life of Jesus. Now his eyes shone and a smile illumined his face showing him to be a handsome man. All the tension had flowed out of him. In its place the flower of trust began to bud and an encounter was beginning — a genuine encounter.

He told me that when he first went to La Paz to work, knowing nothing about Bolivia's capital and not even speaking Spanish, he was welcomed in a hospice run by a community of sisters. I had spent some nights in that same hospice myself, even though they preferred to shelter Indians from the high plateau. We were now buddies who had shared the same shelter, experienced the same homelessness, accomplices so to speak. He shared with me his anxiety during that first night in La Paz, his first days, the exploitation at work, the feeling of being lost in that big city.

As we were excitedly talking, the mother reappeared with a plate of rice, a fried fish, and some delicious Andean potatoes. Her smile said more than any words. The father said,

"Eat. You must be hungry after such a long journey. I know what it's like. I've been there too. You have to keep up your strength."

I accepted thankfully. His words kept echoing in my heart, "I know what it's like. I've been there too."

Everybody sat on the tree stumps they use for chairs and the father continued his stories about work in La Paz, about his first visit to a church one morning early with one of the sisters. The children listened with fascination. He probably had not told them much of this before. We talked until late.

Suddenly the father called Simón to him and said something in Aimara. The boy's face shone and he cast a furtive glance at me, a look rich with promise. He went into the house.

When he came back the father said, "It's late. Time for bed. Let's go."

I looked towards my little shelter in the pig sty but the father said, "No, not there. You're going to sleep in the house with us. Come on."

Simón took my hand and, happy and smiling, he led me into the house. It was small with just one room, a floor of earth and a roof of straw. In a corner was a mattress for me. In another corner was a wood fire, obviously the "kitchen." The house had no furniture, just mats laid on the ground. They did have warm quilts for covering.

Pointing to the corner the father said, "You can sleep there. The quilt is warm. At least this one night you won't be cold."

I thought of refusing saying that really I'd prefer a mat to a mattress but, seeing the light shining from every face I knew that I ought to accept, that this was a very special night and not only for me.

At the family's request we lit a candle and prayed briefly, ending with the Our Father which all of them knew.

Everyone lay down and the mother put out the lamp. In the dark under my warm quilt and feeling so welcome, my tired body fell immediately into deep sleep.

This wonderful night made up for so many that were spent fighting cold and wind. And I received this gift through the insistence of a little boy whose heart was the size of his sacred lake, Lake Titicaca, a boy worthy of his noble ancestors.

We woke at dawn. After coffee and home-made buns I said goodbye. Though my heart felt a bit heavy, a song proclaimed the beauty of what I had just experienced.

Édivan, wise and playful, and Vitoria, quiet yet talkative

In the sertão,
May, 1993

The adult world is so strangely removed from the world of children. Where went their innocence, their simplicity, their purity, their trust? Jesus said it so well — that we have to rediscover these qualities of the child that lie dormant in the hearts of adults.

Two encounters, just one day apart, showed me the truth of what Jesus said.

It was about eleven in the morning when I arrived at a hamlet in this region of the sertão. There was just one street. At the end of it was a pretty little chapel. At eleven o'clock in the sertão the sun is already scorching hot. At this time people stop work until the hottest part of the day is over. The door of the church had a large overhang offering generous and welcome shade. There I sat down, welcomed by the one who lives in a place like this. The chapel was closed, which is usual unfortunately.

Little by little my weariness left me. The street was totally deserted. I expect everyone was indoors, retreating from the heat.

I took the bible from my knapsack and my icon of the Trinity from my shirt pocket. At the locked door of this church I joined my prayer to that of all the men and women who worshipped here, who lived in this community. I offered the life of each one individually with all its pains and sufferings, hopes and joys.

While I was praying psalm 87, a song of unity in the Church, a boy carrying a ball came out of a house on the corner, a pretty house painted blue. He came over to me and asked, "Are you resting?"

"Yes, I am. It's nice here."

"What book is that?"

"It's the bible, the Word of God."

"But if you're praying why don't you go into the chapel?"

"I would like to, but it's closed."

"I know who has the key. His name is Luís. His is that pink house behind the bakery."

Just then a woman called the boy — his mother probably — and he went. Nothing happens by chance, I reflected. Now asking for a key, which I do sometimes, means always to be identified whereas to my mind a pilgrim should pass through simply, leaving no trace, no footsteps, merely the freshness of a breeze. But this boy was sent, his words were a sign. I collected my things and went to find Luís.

That was easy. The hamlet had only one bakery and not many pink houses. I announced myself and the man came to the door. I told him I would like to pray in the chapel. Not waiting for me to finish asking, he said coldly,

"Do you have a letter from the padre?"

I smiled. The boy hadn't put such a question to me. The padre lives some forty kilometers distant. It wouldn't be easy for a pilgrim to come equipped with such letters. I said no. He then became aggressive:

"Without express orders from the padre, I open to nobody. And anyway what do you want to do there? You say you want to pray but nowadays young people don't pray anymore. Especially those like you! They hang out in bars. I don't open. Afterwards you'll steal and I have to answer for it."

With that, he closed the door. He was no more ready to open his house to me than the church. There was no point in insisting. I went back to the chapel door with its shade porch, more welcoming than Luís. Opening the bible I resumed praying.

Moments later the boy was back, still carrying a ball. He asked, "Well, aren't you going to pray in the chapel?"

"It seems not. Luís doesn't want to open."

"But a church is for praying!"

"Yes, it is. God says it is a 'house of prayer.' "

"Grown-ups are all miserable."

I smiled. The purity of this child compensated for the hardness of some adults. I asked,

"What is you name, son?"

"Édivan. You want to play ball?"

"Yes, I do."

Such an invitation I always regard as a door opening. He showed me how he and his friends played ball here on the porch. He was more skilled and experienced and beat me. But a stern voice from the direction of his house interrupted our game:

"Édivan, come home."

He gave me a sad smile, took the ball and said,

"It's always like this. The grown-ups are so boring. I wish just once I could play without having to stop right away. Tchau! And have a good trip."

Édivan left and I was alone once more.

I rested there a while and when the sun began to decline I left. But I was blessed and sent on my way by Édivan.

One day later I saw off in the distance another community much like the one the day before: a single long street and on a rise, the church. It appeared to be open although I couldn't be sure of this what with the blinding light of the sun. Only when I got nearer did I see that it really was open. Blessing of God! I climbed the steps slowly, took off my hat and entered.

In the dim light inside I could see nothing until my eyes adjusted. The vigil light told me that the Blessed Sacrament was reserved here and that someone was awaiting me. I went to the front and knelt. The silence, the dim light, the vigil lamp all spoke of the great mystery. I had only to allow it to envelope me.

After a long period of silence I heard tiny steps and muffled laughter.

Two little girls were playing hide-and-seek behind pillars, and glancing furtively at me. I smiled at their innocence, their purity. Then I joined their game, hiding my face in my hands every time they looked at me. Now their laughter echoed unabashed.

The less shy of the two came and sat beside me, the other a little farther back. I spoke with the first but it was the other that answered:

"She's mute. She can't talk."

"Is she? And what is her name?"

"Vitoria. . . ."

Vitoria — mute but a talker like one seldom sees. With rapid gestures she transmitted her questions to her friend who translated them for me.

The questions came at me rapid fire, tumbling over each other in their haste. Vitoria, the mute, directed the conversation. From where had I come, where was I going, why was I walking, why was I in the church, why did I kneel. She wanted to know it all! This encounter with these two girls, so entirely unforeseen, so happy and so lively in the silence and dimness of that church, had in it all the charm of mystery.

Vitoria would have stayed longer had her friend not urged her insistently to go for lunch. In the silence that followed their departure I offered up to the Father the lives of these two girls. The purity of heart that Vitoria displayed called me — and calls me still — to be myself more trusting, more innocent. What we can learn from the hearts of children!

But the silence didn't last long. In fifteen minutes Vitoria was back, a big smile lighting up her face. She had brought me a plate of rice and beans. I don't know if her mother sent it or Vitoria was offering me her own lunch. An inner voice prompted me, saying it was indeed her own lunch.

We left the church and sat down on the sidewalk along the shady side of the building. I ate slowly savoring each morsel of this meal. I shared it with Vitoria, and eating together only added to the value of this encounter. Her offering was becoming more and more beautiful.

It was now nearly one in the afternoon and students from the school immediately behind the church stopped on their way to classes. Suddenly there were a few dozen, all curious about us. Vitoria sat close to me, radiantly happy.

Then came an elderly lady, all distrustful, in marked contrast to the joy of these children. I wished her good afternoon but she made no reply.

The school bell sounded and all the pupils vanished. Only Vitoria and the old woman were still there. Vitoria picked up her plate and hurried home and the woman left.

I returned to the church eager for a prolonged time of contemplation. I knelt where I had knelt before, before the one who always awaits us. In the presence of the Lord I had met so many children and had even conversed with one who was mute. . . . I let the silence of recollection descend over me.

But again there were steps in the church. These steps were heavy, tired, not the lively, happy steps of those little girls. A door closed, a window was banged shut, an iron latch sliding into place echoed through the church. . .and then a voice spoke:

"If anybody's in there, come on out, because I'm locking up!"

As I left, I wasn't at all surprised to see the same woman that I had seen at the end of our lunch. I thanked her for having found the church open and wished her a good day. No response.

As I was walking off I heard two women say,

"How come she's closing the church so early today. Surely it's not time yet."

The other added, "It's always open the whole day. Perhaps the caretaker has to go somewhere this afternoon."

But I know this was not the reason for closing early.

I recalled Édivan's comment,

"Grown-ups are so tiresome."

For Édivan grown-ups meant the "adult" grown-ups, those who had lost the heart of their childhood. That would make them, unfortunately, "miserable," even "mean."

Vitoria and Édivan. . . . One wise and playful; the other mute but talkative.

The kingdom of God belongs to them. We can enter there only if and when we will be invited by them, because they are its owners. . . .

Jesus said,

> *"Let the little children come to me. . .*
> *because theirs is the kingdom of God."*

(Mk 10: 14)

Would you like some mangos?

Piaui,
October, 1992

The high sertão is genuine desert here on the border between Piaui and Ceará. One can walk leagues and leagues without seeing one green leaf, except of course the mandacaru and its fellow cacti. Leagues and leagues without seeing a single house or even just one person. To say nothing of finding water. . . .

It was walking thus some two, three hours when, ascending a small rise, I heard the shouts and laughter of children. How wonderful! The hope of meeting them filled me with new life. The hot sun and my dry throat roused in me also the hope that I would find a glass of water for my brother, my body.

I saw their house, strong, well-rooted in the soil, built to last for centuries. And all around it was the miracle of water: flowers, green trees, a plot of manioc. It takes only a bit of water to make the sertão flourish.

The children were playing in the middle of the road — three girls and two boys. When they saw me coming — a strange vagabond with a hat and a sack on his shoulder — they screamed and ran to their porch for safety.

Oh, that cursed story that unthinking adults tell children about "that man with the sack" that carries off children! It only serves to traumatize them, to create mistrust, to fill their innocent hearts with a useless fear, a false and harmful fear. . . . Such stories even cause terror at times and do damage to their innocence and purity.

I didn't want to increase their fright and resolved to pass by on the far side of the road without stopping. I was stressed and pained by their fear, and though I was very thirsty, I figured this was the best course to take.

But just as I came abreast of the house a little girl's voice called,

"Would you like some mangos?"

I stopped, speechless with surprise. The children were all standing on the porch quietly looking at me.

The oldest girl said, "We have lots. You can suck some and take some more with you."

The littlest one, the one who had spoken first, ran into the house saying,

"I'm going to get the mangos."

After the heat of the sun, the coolness of the porch shade was refreshing. I sat down among the children and soon felt quite at home.

The little girl came back with a dish full of mangos. On her face was a look of satisfaction that she couldn't disguise. Her mother came out too with a smile born of such profound goodness that there was no need for words.

"Good day, sir," she said. "Take a seat."

One of the boys ran off to find me a stool and the mother, turning to one of the girls said,

"He must be thirsty. Bring him some water — out of that second pot we filled last night."

I stayed more than an hour under that welcoming porch roof. Between mangos I told the children stories. And they taught me one of their games, one where a panther is trying to catch one of their lambs. Not so far from reality as there are really panthers here in the sertão. The little girls laughed with delight when I lost the game. Good thing too, because it meant the lambs would be safe.

The mother spoke of the drought scourging the land these past two years. All the wells and dugouts round about had dried up. Only in the basin where they lived was there still some water, but their well, too, threatened to dry up. For this year they could plant only these plots around the house. Her husband had gone to Terezina where he had found work as a stone mason's helper. He was able to come home every two weeks which made more bearable the pain of separation. Many others had gone to Brasilia and even farther, to São Paulo. No one knew when they might return, or even if they might return. . . . "When the green of your eyes is reflected in the fields," says the song. . . . "When will that be?"

But the green of hope and the tenderness of love have not vanished from this house. That precious pearl, innocence and purity, has been safeguarded here and handed on from the parents to the children. A light shines in the eyes of everyone here, the light of the beatitudes.

It was Cidinha, the littlest girl, who asked if I had a bible. On hearing that I had, she asked in a voice that brooked no denial,

"Oh! then read a little to us."

I chose this section:

> *"So Jesus called a child and had it stand in front of them, and said, 'I assure you that unless you become like children, you will never enter the kingdom of heaven. The greatest in the kingdom of heaven is the one who humbles himself and becomes like this child.' "*
>
> *(Mt 18: 2-4)*

Once back on the road I kept hearing that little voice call, "Would you like some mangos?" The weight of the mangos in my knapsack lightened my steps and spoke of the Love that had made its dwelling in these hearts.

PART II

Pilgrim
of the streets
and sidewalks

"Come, sleep with me. . . ."

Roberto, Cruz de la Sierra

"Stay with us."

Cabeludo, Recife

"The poor constantly appeal to the church, calling her to conversion, because many of them realize in their lives the evangelic values of solidarity, service, simplicity and readiness to welcome God's gift."

Puebla 1147

The miracle of welcome. . . . Have I the right to describe it? But reality already whispers it: from arriving in a big city at night, not knowing anyone, to not knowing a word of the local language, I have never slept alone on the streets. Moreover, I've never asked to join these "street sufferers." On the contrary, I've always been invited. Invited by them, welcomed by those who do not have homes to sleep in. It's the miracle of welcome. . . .

Roberto knew how to make the stranger welcome, to invite him to share his "home" in Santa Cruz de la Sierra. Carlos knew it, too, in Lima; and Cabeludo, Katia and so many more; Cinira in São Paulo, Titi in La Paz. They opened the doors of their hearts to welcome the stranger, the vagabond, the one not expected. . . .

Happy are they. . .in the Kingdom of Heaven. They will be the first to be welcomed, will receive the first places.

Carlos of Lima

Lima
February, 1990

I arrived in Lima at dawn, four days ago. I travelled all night perched on top of a freight truck, without ever once closing my eyes.

The driver left me off on the outskirts of the city. Lima. . . ! The great capital of Peru.

After four weeks of walking from La Paz, crossing the Andes and the southern Peruvian desert, this sudden plunge into an urban society was harsh and demanding.

One's first day in a new city is usually a day of discovery, but it is above all else a call to trust and self-abandonment.

Already that first day I encountered various street people, "street sufferers" they call themselves. I asked for alms at the door of a church with an old beggar, happy to have him for company. He told me where I could eat for almost nothing, in a "restaurant" for street people.

As I was exhausted from my night without sleep, I wanted to rest in some square in the afternoon. I didn't know in advance that this square was a favourite hang-out for street children. I made friends with them readily and we played and talked the whole afternoon. What a delightful first contact!

Late in the afternoon I participated in a celebration of the Eucharist, offering to the most Holy Trinity my time in Lima. When I left the church it was already dark. I was alone, still half lost in this city so new to me. How would my night be!

I allowed my steps to be my guide. The street children had disappeared. The old beggar had disappeared. I wandered about, searching for I don't know what, when I found myself — where else?! — in Lima's central square, surrounded by the governor's palace, city hall, the cathedral, and other important buildings. And everywhere military police. That's because Peru was having a presidential election and various anarchist and terrorist movements were sowing fear, shedding the blood of innocent victims.

It was already ten o'clock. Overcome by exhaustion, I sat down on the cathedral steps. I felt the city pressing in on me, threatening me. The street lighting, though the lamps were many and strong, did little to dissipate the dark and menacing shadows of the night. I felt so alone, so much in need of support.

Just then there appeared in the square a man, strong and well-built, wearing merely patched pants held up by a bit of string. He was shirtless and carried a sack on his back.

He was talking loudly and gesticulating in all directions. He came up to me, stopped and said,

"Are you new here?"

"Yes, I've just come."

"What!! Talk louder!!" He said this in shouts.

"I've just come," I repeated, more loudly.

"So then, you're new. That's what I said."

The man put down his sack on one of the steps and sat down near me. He spoke about the political situation, the corruption, the terrorism. He spoke so loudly I feared the military police might suddenly intervene.

But then he abruptly changed subjects: "It's clear to me you have no idea where you'll sleep tonight. Come with me. I'll show you the ropes."

More than an invitation, this was a command, and so I went with him. I picked up my sack, he picked up his, and we went "house hunting." We studied marquees, building entrances, church doorways. I was so exhausted from my sleepless night and the long day, that it cost me a great effort not to collapse during this endless wandering of the streets.

And finally we ended up where we had started, in Lima's main square! It was past midnight. Only the soldiers and military police armed with machine guns and other weapons thankfully unknown to me, remained in the square. I wondered if they would permit us to sleep here.

But my companion didn't give them a second thought:

"So then, we need to choose a spot. It doesn't matter where because they're all dangerous. Lima is riddled with violence. Much violence. You know what you'd best do? Stay with me, right here. I sleep nearby."

Saying this he gestured toward the cathedral steps. I could hardly control my stupefaction. . . .

"Right here?"

"If I say here, it means here, but not the cathedral steps. No, in the doorway of this palace. It's the bishop's."

And really there it was, an imposing building in the shadow of the governor's palace — the bishop's palace.

Not giving me time to reply he hoisted his sack to his shoulder and he said,

"Come on. It's late and you're falling asleep standing up. Oh, I nearly forgot, I'm Carlos. And you, what's your name?"

"Henrique."

"How's that?" Again it was a shout.

"Henrique!"

"Oh! Henrique!"

Carlos, you represent the tender mercy of God. You knew how to open your house, your house without doors, to welcome an unknown, a vagabond. You saw how lost he was in the dark shadows of the great city.

"Happy are you who. . . . In the Father's Kingdom you will have the first places."

Titi, from the flower market of La Paz

La Paz
November, 1989

The mystery of welcome and of encounters! This second night in La Paz, how I was blessed by the Father!

I slept — if one can call it that! — the first night in a small square amongst a group of drunks who didn't sleep the whole night through. It was a night full of excitement, merely lively at first. But it finally turned violent, a fight with broken bottles.

This second night I didn't know where to sleep, but I had little desire to return to the group I slept with last night. I was hoping for a more tranquil night, a night that would grant me at least a few hours of sleep.

Not many people sleep on the sidewalks of La Paz because the nights are cold here, high up in the Andes. Most street people seek out abandoned homes or some corner sheltered from the wind, a hiding place known only to themselves. That's why a newcomer to a city like La Paz is a little lost at first.

At ten o'clock I was still in St. Francis Square near the city center. I passed by the flower market, a succession of stalls deserted at this hour. In front of one of the stalls were heaped the now discarded flowers. I looked among the wilted blossoms for one that still displayed her beauty.

After a vain search I spied a man sitting in front of one of the stalls. He eyed me with wide open eyes and a smile that brightened his face and illumined the night. He held two roses, two red roses in full bloom.

He gestured for me to approach and when I drew near he offered me a flower.

I accepted the rose, the flower I had been hoping to find. I dropped my cardboard and knapsack and fell to my knees in front of him, in front of this living icon.

O tenderness of the Trinity! If we only knew how great is God's hope for us — a hope that goes beyond, infinitely beyond, what we can think or imagine. It wasn't some flower scavenged from the garbage that the Trinity wanted to offer me this night but a red rose received along with a welcome look and a gentle smile.

I was speechless. The man invited me to sit down beside him. I arranged my cardboard in silence and sat down.

After a while I said, "Thank you, friend. The rose is fragrant and beautiful."

"Yes, yes."

"It has transformed the night for me."

"Yes, yes."

We conversed for some time but he could only say, "Yes, yes," accompanied each time with a double inclination of his head. I was ready to dub him "Yes, yes."

"Friend, what's your name?" I asked.

I thought he would say "Yes, yes," but he smiled and said distinctly, "Titi."

Titi! It's the only word he said that night apart from "Yes, yes."

Titi fascinated me. Beyond (way beyond) our verbal language he communicated the wonder-filled world in which he lives.

After an hour of gestures, words and smiles, Titi suddenly lowered his head. Now I no longer saw that luminous look, that radiant smile. When he raised his head once more, his countenance had changed. He looked worried, a bit fearful. After a moment's hesitation he asked me by way of gestures:

"Would you sleep here with me?"

I nodded my head in agreement. Then his eyes opened up still wider and his smile returned. He jumped up in happy joy, arranged the cardboard for both of us and opened up his big blanket to protect us from the cold. We lay down side by side. He looked at me as if to make sure I was really there and then pulled the blanket over his head. He fell asleep on the instant.

It took me a while to fall asleep. The Andean cold had disappeared. The warmth of Titi's welcome had banished it. Two red roses at our heads were proclaiming what words couldn't transmit. The starry heavens made me think of the Psalmist's praise:

> *"Day unto day takes up the story*
> *And night unto night makes known the message.*
> *No speech, no word, no voice is heard*
> *Yet their span goes forth through all the earth,*
> *Their words to the utmost bounds of the world.*
>
> (Psalm 19 (18): 3-5)

Without speech, without words. . . . Just red roses. . . .

Twice Titi awoke. He sat up, rubbed his eyes and gazed at me intently as if to certify that I was really still there. Then he lay down again and slept peacefully.

I, too, fell into a profound sleep. A little before dawn Titi shook me awake. He was sitting up. His countenance was once more bright with that happy smile and wide-eyed innocence. With arm outstretched he pointed upward with his index finger and said, "Yes, yes."

I looked, it was snowing. The flakes were falling gently. Our blanket was already white. We sat there a while snug in the blanket, protected a little by the roof of a flower stall. We watched the dance of the snowflakes.

The night had become magical, surreal. A red rose, my encounter with

Titi, this sharing of gestures and smiles, the invitation to sleep there, the starry sky, the deep sleep and now this dance of snowflakes crowning a night of marvels.

The snowflakes seemed to sing Paul's thanksgiving hymn:

> *"God, through the power with which he acts in us, can accomplish more than we ask for or can imagine; to him be given glory in the church and in Jesus Christ through all generations, forever, Amen!"*

(Eph 3: 20-21)

"It's not a question of merely giving. And certainly not of tossing something at the poor in contempt. No, it's a question of sharing."

Cinira of São Paulo

Love always knows how to make of an encounter a dividing and a sharing.

Love doesn't throw things at one, doesn't humiliate a person. Love doesn't make line-ups, and doesn't order you to line up. Love doesn't ignore you as a person.

Love offers itself. It ennobles. It dances a roundelay in a circle open to the wind and it invites everyone to join in. Love looks for an encounter with another.

Love simply loves — and waits, even waits patiently, to be loved.

Now those groups in big cities who make their rounds at night doling out food to those who suffer hunger — how can they do that without being motivated by love, love which knows how to share, be in solidarity and communion. Should these characteristics not be transparent at the moment of giving out soup or bread?

Or is it perhaps not love that motivates these folks on their evening rounds?

The hearts of street people are sensitive and vulnerable. Every humiliation strikes more deeply at their wounds, already bleeding. On the other hand, each smile and hug, each name known and spoken, is like balm on those wounds.

How can we learn to see life as Cinira sees it, live it as she lives it?

The food-as-charity circuits of Recife — and of so many other cities

Recife,
July, 1992

Recife. . .

Already since my first night here (such is the miracle of welcome!) I have been sleeping with a group in a street with furniture stores. . . . Such irony! Their doors and windows are all of glass and we lie down on the cold concrete in front of all these beds and mattresses. We also eat from tin cans scavenged from garbage dumps, in full view of well-equipped kitchens and restaurants.

Jesus once told this story:

"There was a rich man dressed in purple and fine linen, who gave daily banquets.

A poor man named Lazarus, all covered with sores used to be brought to the rich man's door hoping to eat the bits of food that fell from the rich man's table."

(Lk 16: 19-21)

Most of our group of ten are alcoholics. Either because of having drunk too much, or of not having anything to drink, the nights are full of threats, of weeping, of tension with no concern for the lateness of the hour. Sometimes even violence breaks out. One's sleep is constantly interrupted.

Occasionally charitable groups, principally spiritists, make their rounds with coffee and bread, or soup. But none of them takes the time to sit down and talk with the people. We don't know their names, and they don't know ours. It is all so anonymous, so impersonal.

We have the impression that they want to hand out the food and get away as quickly as possible. Are they afraid?

Afraid of a fellow human being? Of an encounter? Encounters are demanding, it's true. Meeting a suffering brother or sister can lead one along paths as yet unknown. . . . It could even cause one to risk one's own life. . . . Would I have the courage to go "to the very end" to love to the end? (Jn 13: 1)

The street people often have had nothing to eat the whole day and they welcome this hot soup. But they are hungry for so much more, for friendship, for conversation, for having someone listen to them. They want to be treated as people and not just "hungry mouths."

When these "philanthropists" roar off with the cars with which they so suddenly invaded our space they leave us with some bitterness of heart. The soup was good, yes, but they squandered the chance for an encounter, and encounter is a chance for mutual enrichment.

Sharing the night with Cabeludo

Recife,
July, 1992

Our group gets along very well! Dona Lourdes, Cabeludo, Mario, and our other companions are all very loyal to each other. We have made of this bit of sidewalk "our corner" for sleeping. When we arrive here at night some are already expecting us and we wait for the rest.

It warms our hearts to see each other, to give a hug, to tell about our day, to share a dry bun. Our steps hurry as we come near to "our corner."

One night I stayed quite late with the street children in the city center and arrived at "our corner" only at one in the morning. With my cardboard under my arm I regarded all those bodies stretched out on the sidewalk, delivered into the hands of healing sleep, but also unprotected, exposed to all kinds of violence. There lay Neguinha alongside her friend; old Roberto in his corner. . . . Empty cans lying around suggested that soup had been brought and I remembered that I had eaten nothing the whole day except a bun this morning. My stomach suddenly contracted into knots.

We sleep in the entrance of a store and the overhang accommodates only eight persons. I saw right away that all eight spaces were occupied. I would have to sleep in a neighboring entrance unprotected by an overhang. It was the rainy season, and getting drenched during the night was a distinct possibility.

But Cabeludo was awake. "Oh, you've arrived, Henrique! But you're awfully late."

"Yes, I spent time with a group downtown. How was your day?"

"Like always — nothing much to do. Lie down here. You must be tired." He pointed to a place beside him with cardboard already spread out over the cold concrete.

"But," I said, "Isn't that already someone's place?"

"Nobody's. It looks like rain, and so I saved this spot for you. It's no fun getting rained on during the night."

And from the head-end he produced a can along with a bun, "We had soup — tasty, too! I kept some for you. It came with bread."

Such tenderness!. . .

The night circuit in Salvador. . .
. . .and a soup of chicken legs

Salvador,
December, 1994

They stopped. . . . They stopped but I didn't get up. They clapped their hands, but I stayed lying. I didn't get up and I won't get up. I'm tired. So tired.

Formerly I often did get up. Many, many times I got up. Perhaps I was expecting too much. I would get up to talk. Yes, also to take the soup they were bringing but principally for the chance of an encounter. To meet someone. . .but, maybe I was expecting too much. . .because all I ever got was soup.

So this particular night I didn't get up. I felt so heavy a weight in my heart as I lay there on my cardboard, a weight I couldn't relieve, the weight of humiliation.

The man, white and flabby, kept on trying to get us to jump to his tune. He clapped his hands, strode back and forth along the length of the marquee hollering, "Soup! Soup, everybody!!"

No, I will not line up. And I will not get up either! I'm not "everybody." Nor am I "nobody." I grant that I'm sleeping here on the street, but I'm not a dog, nor am I just a "mouth" that should at least know how to form a line.

I'm a human being, but on this night, lying here on this cardboard, that weight pressing on my heart is telling me the opposite. This burden is crushing my spirit.

The little man never stops. He keeps walking back and forth, gesticulating, shouting. Can he. . . ? But up to now he hasn't spoken to any one of us.

These well-dressed fellows and girls with manicured nails and lipstick — they don't get out of their cars and they look at us through the windows as they would at animals in the zoo. . . .

Their lights invade our space, the metallic paint of their automobiles blinds us with its brilliance. In that third car a tape deck is assaulting our ears with music that comes from beyond our frontiers, is foreign to our culture.

A few go for the soup. They pronounce it tasty, well-flavored. Could be, but I'm not going to sample it. On this night I prefer to be alone with my hunger. It is already my friend having accompanied me the whole day.

Miudinha also did not go to get the soup. She is staying with a fire she made. There, in an oil can, she is boiling a dozen hens' legs that she scavenged at the market. She doesn't even look at the cars. With a stick she stirs the soup in her improvised pot.

From a half-ton truck a sarcastic voice yells, "Would you look at that! Just look what she's cooking. Hey, I'd like to sample your chicken broth!"

But Tanira (Miudinha is just her nickname) doesn't react. She doesn't even give the impression that she has heard. The voice keeps on mocking:

"Soup of cardboard, eh? A little cardboard in warm water. Gotta be tasty, not so?"

I feel paralyzed. . .impotent. But Tanira quietly continues stirring in her can. She says nothing. There are silences, however, that are more eloquent than words.

The line of cars left. The fat man left. The voices fell silent. Those over-powering lights disappeared. Tanira's little fire once more lights up our space with its dancing little flames. There, at least, is life.

Gradually, with silence restored, I feel the oppressive burden begin to lift from my heart. I even make the effort to get up, but I'm tired. So tired.

Tanira takes the tin from the fire and speaking softly, says,

"Now that they have gone, we can eat." I concluded that for her the soup that the cars brought was not really a meal. And she's right. A meal is a meeting place, a place of communion. But what the cars brought was not "encounter" nor any sort of "communion." Just soup. Soup and a large dose of humiliation.

But now it's time for dinner. Tanira divides her food, to each one a sin-gle chicken leg and a bit of broth. No salt and no pepper. No oil, nothing. Just chicken legs and water.

Suddenly my weariness leaves me. I am seated at Tanira's dinner. From this soup I will eat. At this festive meal my heart can rejoice.

Thank you, Miudinha. . . .

Celebrating a reunion with Pirá

Salvador,
November, 1991

I got to Salvador just before nightfall, the hour when the equatorial sun prepares to set, offering to one who knows how to wonder a symphony of color. This gentle hour before dark is already cool. Walking along Salvador's seashore in the warm sand, with a light breeze caressing my face, and gazing at the palm trees proudly showing off their coconuts, I rejoiced again in this "Brazil-as-Paradise," where nature offers itself exu-berantly.

But "Brazil-as-Paradise" is reserved to a few, to tourists and to the upper classes. At the other extreme is "Brazil-as-Hell." That's where the street people live, children as well as adults. That's where the people of the slums live. It's a hell ruled by misery, by violence, by prostitution, by drugs.

I arrived at the city center in time for the eucharist at the monastery of St. Benedict. Participating in the liturgy with the Benedictines is most gratifying during these weeks that I am spending with the street people of Salvador.

When I left the church night had already fallen. I scavenged some cardboard from a heap of garbage and even found a quarter loaf of bread halfway between fresh and stale. After that I simply let my steps take me where they would.

At the square of Piedade, near the church, I met Pirá, the man who had welcomed me last year here on the streets of Salvador. We had slept together in the doorway of the church of Piedade sharing the same cardboard. Those weeks of living with Pirá and the "Piedade bunch," with Jacobina, with Dona Jaqueline, Dona Zefinha, with Luciano. . . , they had marked me profoundly. How happy I was to meet them again.

This reunion called for a party. Seated on our cardboards in the church entrance we exchanged news. There was so much to share, the happenings of a whole year, its joys and its tears, who had come and who had gone. . .gone down other roads or even to the house of our Father.

A party must have a meal and we shared what we had: I the bread I had found in the garbage, Pirá some over-ripe mangos he had obtained from somewhere. We divided the bread and sucked the mangos.

Food from the garbage? Rotten mangos? But this was food for a feast. It had the taste of friendship, of fidelity. Bread shared carries with it smiles and joy.

And so, in the heart of this "Brazil-as-Hell" it is not the "Brazil-as-Paradise" I am coming back to. No, it is the kingdom of our heavenly Father that is being realized here. The Christian, the man and woman of faith, is not called to reenter "Paradise Lost" but is invited to help build the Father's kingdom.

And it is in the hearts of the poor that one finds the coming of that reign.

"Happy are you who are poor,
for yours is the kingdom of God."

(Lk 6: 20)

Glicerio's Soup

São Paulo,
August, 1992

Cinira, a street woman of São Paulo, said once,
"Don't just give. And don't throw, either.
It's sharing!
If I have two cakes, I give you one.
If I have one grain of rice, I cut it in half.
That's how I see things
and that's how I live my life."

Cinira shows us the way, the path of salvation for humanity. The road to solidarity is by sharing.

And that's what the street woman, Cinira, teaches us: that we really don't need anything to take that first step. Nor does it matter if the others do it too, or not. What matters is that I myself have the confidence and faith to take this first step. Who knows what this first step will awaken in me?

That's what Cinira says, and that's what Cinira does. Her sensibility, her generous and good heart were born together with the community of sufferers, street people, a group that is known today as Glicerio's soup, well known to the street people of São Paulo.

This soup is prepared by the street people themselves and therein lies a great difference — the whole difference.

Each Wednesday some twenty-five men and women of the street gather under the Glicerio viaduct. After the market closes they scavenge among what's left behind, unsold, thrown on the ground, society's waste. While some do the scavenging, others wash, cut away what has begun to rot. Still others light a fire using wood lying about.

"Our first soup was made in a twenty liter oil can," recounts Cinira. Today the water boils in three large kettles filled with beets, pumpkin, carrots, potatoes, celery, onion, green leaves and seasoning. Sometimes even chicken. The aroma of soup pervades the viaduct. From being merely a dusty and noisy place it is now cozy and welcoming. Street people arrive, talk in small groups. The soup is almost ready. . . .

Everybody is aware of it: here one doesn't line up. Queueing up is what folks do when they are outside their own place, where it's strange. One doesn't do it at home. Lining up isn't human, it's anonymous, individualist. In a queue one sees only the backs of the people in front. On the street we should make such lines?! For Glicerio's soup, the street people's soup, one does not line up.

No! We all sit in a huge circle. A circle is communitarian. In a circle you can see everyone's face. In a circle you feel that you are indeed somebody, part of a family.

When the kettles arrive they are placed in the middle of the circle and some volunteers, street people themselves, serve the others. Nobody needs to get up. All are served where they sit. It's all done so calmly, no shoving, no chance of queue jumping when no queue exists.

The time of distributing food is considered sacred. It is the hour for sharing, the hour for service.

This soup has its unique flavor. . . . It's not like getting your soup already in its can, given you on the sidewalk by people who don't want to bother getting to know you as a person. Here with Glicerio's soup you don't have to lower your head. And furthermore it's important to gather the ingredients yourself, to light the fire, to prepare the soup, and, even though it's underneath a viaduct, to serve the others. With Glicerio's soup one recovers a sense of human dignity, of personhood.

As they say here, "This is our soup."

It's a road open to us, not necessarily an example, because no ready-made solution exists. But it is a way, like the way Paul speaks of,

"I will show you a way that surpasses all others."

(1 Cor 12: 31)

It is the path of Love.

Love always knows how to encounter the other in the act of sharing. Always Love thirsts to invent new forms of solidarity, of justice. If we knew how to welcome Love the way Cinira does. . . , if we only knew how to free up space in our lives for Love's hope, for its dream to be realized. . . , there are then many signs like that of Glicerio's soup, signs of Love's bursting into life in every place where suffering is present, in each groan of pain.

"Love's patience never fails."

(1 Cor 13: 7)

The mystery within each of us

"Every man, every woman is a holy story;
all were made in the image of God."

(Liturgical hymn)

God created us in his image, in his image and likeness he created us; man and woman he created us. . . .

And if God, par excellence, is mystery, what shall we say of us created in his image and likeness? Who can guess the unplumbed depths of a heart? Who can see behind the veil into the secret garden of the soul?

In these years in which I have lived with people on the streets and side-walks some men, women and children have marked my story forever. Their mystery evokes another mystery, calls up questions which are the arche-typal questions of all time, of every culture, of every religion.

Dai, the mystery of communication

Salvador,
December, 1991

"Dai" (her real name is Aide), is a mentally deficient woman. She keeps mainly to the square of São Bento in Salvador's upper city. She talks to herself in words without apparent meaning and no coherence. At times her strident shouts fill the square. She dresses in extravagant clothes, some-times very dirty. She calls to people, gesturing wildly. Pedestrians and street sellers go out of her way. Is it from fear, from prejudice, racism, that they judge her? "She's crazy. . . ."

Occasionally I was sitting in the square during one of her crises, pray-ing for her in my heart and hoping that she might approach me so that we might meet. I didn't want to force anything, to impose any kind of rela-tionship, but I trusted that given time an opportunity might arise.

One afternoon I sat writing in the square. I didn't notice when Dai (at that time I didn't yet know her name) came close, then sat down beside me.

110

Without saying a word she tore the pen out of my hand and scribbled up the whole page. I let her do it, in fact the scribbles were quite pretty — I'd have to rewrite the page but that didn't matter — and when she finished, I gave her another sheet.

But then, to my great surprise, she stopped scribbling. Instead she began to write. She would write a few words, never speaking but adding expressive gestures to this mute dialogue:

"I. . .nothing."

"Address, never had."

"5.12.91" (the correct date)

"I not sex maniac."

"I can't take it."

"Age 38."

"Dai." (pointing to herself)

"Not my heart." (pointing to her heart)

She didn't speak a single word all the while that she wrote. But with the many gestures she made between her spurts of writing, this went on a good hour. I kept reading what she wrote out loud, commenting occasionally. To my comments she would indicate yes or no gesturing with her head or a finger.

This first encounter with Dai ended as precipitately as it began. She suddenly got up and left. No glance back, no look, no word of goodbye. . .but she left my pen behind.

After that we met nearly every day. Our friendship grew and little by little she began to speak a few words. She is able to carry on a normal conversation and today we no longer need pen and paper as intermediaries. Trust took root and our meetings resulted in many hours of sharing of experiences. These were interspersed with tears and smiles, punctuated by weeping and by laughter. Entrusting to me episodes of her past she was freeing herself from oppressive shadows and from deep wounds.

Some days ago about mid-day I was returning from São Francisco Convent where I had gone to receive a soup they serve to the poor and when I arrived at São Bento Square I heard a voice shout,

"Henrique, Henrique!!"

There, at the other side of the square was Dai calling me, and not at all discreetly! I walked past the street venders whose looks and silence spoke volumes, and went to sit beside her. She said,

"I was waiting for you. Because you don't take good care of yourself, I have to do it. I begged some food and here it is, for both of us."

"How splendid, Dai! But I just ate at Chico. (That's the people's affectionate name for St. Francis.)

"Ach, that doesn't stick to your ribs! Only rice and beans. . .And they serve you as if you were a dog! Here I have meat, vegetables, macaroni. . .and enough for us both."

Hungry or not, I couldn't refuse.

In the middle of the bench, between us, she put down a piece of cardboard to serve as table cloth. Although it was dirty, it did give a festive air to our meal. While I went to fetch water she made a spoon out of the lid of a can. She separated some of the food from the tin into a plastic bag. Then she handed me the tin along with the spoon she had made. She kept the plastic bag for herself and ate from it with her fingers. And so we shared.

Her eyes shone with inexpressible joy. We ate in silence — but words were not necessary, they would simply detract from the moment. Only silence was able to reveal what was happening: the joy shining in her face was literally transfiguring her.

This meal, the fruit of a complicity born of our brief daily meetings, was a true, authentic celebration. It celebrated human dignity rediscovered — or newly discovered? — of brotherly and sisterly love, of simplicity.

To be invited by Dai. . . . For this it's necessary to possess nothing, even less than she had, to be able to receive from her. To be there with nothing to offer except life, a loving presence that hopes, can that not restore to men and women the dignity of being able to offer, to invite?

Had Dai ever offered a meal to anyone before?

To offer a meal. . .to invite someone to the table of love and communion. . .the bible reports many meals, from Abraham inviting God himself at Mamre to the final banquet with the Lamb of the Apocalypse. Jesus worked his first miracle around a table at a marriage feast, and he left his disciples at Emmaus after the sharing of bread on the feast of the resurrection. And it was at that last meal, on a Thursday night that he "loved to the end," offering himself as food, making of the meal a sacrament. He made himself a beggar of meals:

> *"Behold I stand at the door and knock. If anyone hears my voice and opens the door, I will come into his house and eat with him, and he will eat with me."*
>
> *(Apoc 3: 20)*

Eduardo, victim of alcohol

La Paz,
January, 1990

First encounter

Wednesday I stayed in the city center of La Paz later than usual with a group of street sufferers. It was nearly midnight when I retraced my steps to the old, abandoned mansion just off São Francisco Square. I sleep there with street people. Crossing the square which is always deserted at this hour and in this cold, I saw a man sitting in one of the doorways of the church. He had only a piece of plastic for a cover. Though I had been on the streets of La Paz for over two months I had not seen him before. His body seemed to be all pain and suffering. I sat down beside him. His legs were as though paralyzed. His whole body smelled of alcohol, of urine and of feces. It was the smell of rot, a stink. . . . He told me that he could no longer walk and that his whole body, but especially his legs, hurt. I helped him arrange his cardboard and asked if he had been to the hospital.

"Not yet, but I will go tomorrow."

I invited him to sleep with us in the big house where at least there would be protection from the rain, and especially from the icy winds that blow across this square at night. He said he couldn't manage even these two hundred meters from here to the big house and that he preferred to stay alone in the square.

I left him there in the windy square with his piece of plastic. . .whereas I had an old abandoned house to sleep in, a jacket and a blanket. . . .

One could write a book about this big house. It's very old, with two inner courtyards, and a veranda on the first floor. Though now abandoned and in ruins it must once have been a small palace. Now it is occupied by La Paz's underworld. In the courtyards are mini-bars housed in canvas tents. Here customers come to look for prostitutes and for drugs. Some of the ground floor rooms serve as a general sleeping area. One room is full of boxes; another is occupied by a family with I don't know how many children. . . . The street people use the veranda of the first floor as their sleeping quarters. It offers a bit of shelter from the rain, and especially from the wind.

On this particular night a terrible rainstorm swept over La Paz. Strongest in forty-five years, the papers said the next day. Our old house was no match for this deluge. In short order there wasn't a dry spot left for even one person to lie down. The canvas of the mini-bars was ripped to pieces, and the victims of prostitution, women as well as young men, came up onto our veranda. It was the only place left with at least a bit of protection.

Standing there on the veranda, I remembered Eduardo, the fellow I had met in the square. I hoped he would have got himself to some sheltered place because that church entrance offered no protection whatever.

When the storm subsided, about 5 a.m., I went directly to São Francisco Square. Eduardo was there exactly as I had left him, like a statue. He was wet; no, drenched.

I stayed with him that morning. He was too drunk to go to the hospital — they would never have taken him in. I offered him a hot corn drink, but he refused it saying his stomach couldn't take it. Some street alcoholics were hovering about. When I finally left Eduardo, before I had arrived at the other side of the square they were already plying him with this terrible poison.

That's how things stood Thursday, Friday and Saturday. Eduardo began to show more seriously a wish to go to the hospital. I agreed several times to accompany him there, but next day he was again too drunk. I finally began sleeping with him under a nearby marquee, sharing my blanket and his plastic. I secretly hoped I could get him sober enough to be interned, but even so I didn't manage it.

All these days Eduardo lived here at the church door, a prisoner of alcohol. An invisible prison held him captive. A prison without walls and bars, but more secure than the most secure penitentiary in the world. Prisoner of a bottle. . . .

Yesterday, Sunday, a lady gave me clothes for Eduardo: shirt, jacket, pants and a blanket. When I arrived at the square that night I presented it all to him. He was overjoyed, especially with the blanket but with all the clean clothes too. His own clothing was rotten and stinky. He wanted to change immediately but couldn't do it alone. At his request I helped him.

It was then that I discovered how grave his condition was. It was already three weeks since he had eaten as I discovered later. His backside was one open, running wound, filled with pus, blood and feces. The same was true of the calves of his legs. I didn't see how he could keep from screaming with pain. I cleaned the feces from the wounds as well as I could. His wounds were all infected. I wanted to take him directly to the hospital but he was drunk again and I knew they wouldn't accept him.

Eduardo had arrived at the extreme limits of what a body can stand. His last resistance melted away and, weeping, he begged,

"Stay with me tonight. When you're here, I don't drink. And stay tomorrow too. Don't leave me even for a second so that I won't drink. And when I'm better, in the afternoon then take me to the hospital. . . ."

I was simply waiting for a sign for him, a resolution a bit more firm than "I'll go tomorrow. . . ." I agreed without any hesitation.

Today, Monday, it wasn't even necessary to wait till the afternoon. Already at 10 in the morning the lack of alcohol, which acts as an analgesic, increased his suffering to insupportable levels and he begged me to take him to the hospital.

The trip there was an adventure in itself, as Eduardo couldn't walk and with his bad smell and his appearance nobody, absolutely nobody, would help. I asked some people to carry my bag, but their look gave me my answer. As we crossed the square, São Francisco, people got as far away from us as they could. I don't know if our brother Francis has a particular eye out for squares and churches that carry his name, but if so he certainly wept. . . , wept with pain and with compassion.

Getting to the hospital was not easy. Nobody would give us a ride. I finally appealed to a guard. He compelled a bus driver who had refused us, to let us on. The humiliation weighed heavily on us and during the trip we both sat with our heads hanging low and saying not a word.

At the hospital we went straight to the emergency. Thank God, from here on things went better. A doctor and several nurses received us with compassion. They washed Eduardo, showing no contempt. The doctor declared his situation "extremely grave," and interned him immediately.

He is now in the dermatology wing, being cared for by a doctor who was very sympathetic. I was able to speak to her and to introduce Eduardo. She said she would try to find some medicines gratis, as there's a lot to be paid for here even though it's a public hospital.

When I left Eduardo it was already late in the afternoon. He was glad to have a bed, clean linens and good care. But this first night without alcohol will be one prolonged agony, a night of great suffering. Alone on his hospital bed he will have to do battle, to struggle the whole night. The lack of alcohol will be a cross.

I want to visit him daily because I know how important it is for him not to be alone. The doctor said,

"What he'll need most in these first days here is affection, tenderness and care."

This is a doctor who does not view the patient merely as a physical, biological body. Her sensitivity to Eduardo's anguish and affliction gave me peace.

The night is already well advanced and São Francisco Square is deserted. I am writing these lines in the doorway of the church where Eduardo lived these last days, where I met him, where I spent last night with him, and where we still were seated as late as this morning. . . . Here I feel closer to him, communing with the life he lived.

In my final prayer before going to the old house to sleep I presented him to the tenderness of the Trinity. Only God can shelter him and alleviate his pain and distress this first night in the hospital.

"He will cover you with his wings,
you will be safe in his care;
You need not fear any dangers at night,
or the plagues that strike in the dark."

(Ps 91: 4-6)

One week later

I kept visiting Eduardo all this week, bringing him a little food when I could. I tried to get others interested in his situation: his brother, a dentist, for whom he had worked. I visited several persons, gave them the necessary references, told them of Eduardo's pressing needs. . . . But none of them visited him, nor did they help to pay for the medicines he needed.

It was a week of great suffering for Eduardo. First of all physical because of the wide-spread infection. His stomach could no longer accept solid foods. He was incapable of any kind of movement, not even to sit up in bed. Added to all this was the psychological suffering, the lack of alcohol, the loneliness. These first days were a long calvary.

There were other men in Eduardo's ward. Few of them received visitors: just two out of the thirty interned here. At first the men rejected Eduardo. He was "that alcoholic" that had just come, dirty, stinky, someone to avoid, and certainly not someone with whom to strike up a friendship.

Spending the days there with Eduardo, I talked with these men. Stays in the dermatology wing are long and lonely, and so the need to share is all the greater. Most of them are Indians, Quechuas or Aimaras from the plateau, the interior of Bolivia. They have no one here in the capital to visit them. I listen to their stories, bring them news from the city. . . . Our friendship begins to grow.

Some play checkers, and I occasionally join in. As Eduardo likes to play too, I asked one day if I might borrow the board to play with him. They agreed and he and I played together.

Gradually their prejudices diminished and now they already fetch water for him (he still can't get up) and do other favors. Eduardo now plays checkers with them regularly and today the whole ward is engaged in a tournament.

It's just a little thing, a grain of sand. But the kingdom of heaven is constructed with little grains of sand.

One week later

Eduardo has been in the hospital two weeks now and has to stay in the dermatology wing at least to the end of March. Two months more. . . . His sores need a lot of time and care to heal entirely. He is eating better and has gained a few kilos. His face is changing and now is occasionally lit up with a smile.

Now I'm beginning to worry about when he leaves the hospital. A recuperation home for alcoholics has already accepted him. I managed this with the help of Alcoholics Anonymous. Some friends offered to visit him and to bring him there when he was ready to be discharged. Will Eduardo have the will power to stay sober? Will his wish to leave off drinking and living on the street be stronger than the urge to drink? I can only hope and confide him to the tender love of the Trinity.

From his hospital bed Eduardo told me one day in confidence,

"You know, I never got used to life on the street. It's not for me. If I want to start over I have to stop drinking."

It's the first step, the open door, a hope.

May God help him, give him the strength to rise up, to be reborn. Eduardo is young, just forty-five and he can start over. Pray for him.

A present from God

God gave me the finest present today, indeed over many days, through Eduardo. After these weeks in the hospital, I was visiting him as I do every day. Seated beside him on his bed, he put his hand on my knee and said,

"Just one. We two — just one."

Barbosa, the unknown wiseman

Arapiraca,
May, 1933

Night had already enveloped the city of Arapiraca in the interior of Alagoas, when I arrived. I thought it would be a small place, but I underestimated the importance of this "tobacco capital." I was tired from the many leagues I had travelled this day and the city center and church square, the place I always head to first when coming to a strange city, seemed to retreat in front of my steps. Finally I arrived at a square, well lit and lively. A huge white building with a high cruciform tower dominated the square. Of course, it was the church, the church I was longing to find. But then I felt a cold shiver in my spine — a fence surrounded it. The pretension, especially of that tower in the form of a cross dampened the joy of my arrival.

The building couldn't even offer me its steps as a resting place, locked, fenced and forbidden. An open church is so welcoming!! My greatest pleasure in arriving in a community is to go immediately to the church either to enter it, or if it is locked because of the lateness of the hour, to sit on its steps. . . , to feel myself welcomed there, welcomed by the people that worship in it, by Jesus. . . , to thank the sweet Trinity for the day, for the journey, for the people I met. . . , to give my tired body a sweet and gentle rest.

I sat down. I let the coolness of the night permeate my sweaty, tired, dusty body. Gradually my tiredness lessened and I began to pay attention to the life of the square.

There were many young people in school uniforms. They were happy and lively, returning from classes, talking and playing in small groups, eating lunches. They were probably from neighboring villages and were waiting for transport home.

They gave the square a festive, jovial tone. The place was theirs and they took full possession. I don't know how I managed to find a place to sit when I arrived. There were no empty places left, not one.

In front of me were three benches arranged in a semi-circle. A man came into the square and headed straight towards them. There was something arresting about him.

He was dressed in layers of clothes, all dark and dirty and carried two cloth sacks packed full. What was in them only he knew. The sacks had once been white but now were caked with grime. He carried two brooms under one arm, making him even more unusual.

The young people seemed to know him well and immediately cleared a place for him to sit. It was probably his regular place. They teased him a bit but he paid no attention. He just talked to himself. He had a bushy beard, mixed black and white and an impressive wig, a beautiful gray in color which could have given him the air of a wise man come from afar had he given it the least bit of attention. Apart from his visible neglect of appearance, however, one could read in his eyes and his general demeanor that he attached no importance to the teasing of the young people, that he had achieved a quiet harmony of spirit.

After a few deep sighs, he took a broom and began to sweep the square. He was very careful about it, leaving the ground immaculate. He gathered the dust, the papers and plastic cups the young people had left behind into the square's garbage containers.

Another group of young people began to tease him. They tried to provoke him with stupid comments, remarks that showed no respect, that only revealed the low level of their conversation. They would say things like, "Who knows the story of the pig-sweep?" They even threw things on the ground he had just swept clean. Quietly he went back and swept the area again, not commenting, indeed hardly noticing these humiliations.

He swept as though it were a job he had to do, and do well. He dedicated himself to his work with great care, giving it an importance that only he understood.

My curiosity was awakened and I felt I would like to get to know him. Something beautiful radiated from this man. I sensed that there was a treasure hidden in this mysterious person.

A bus started its motor and honked. The young people grabbed their texts and exercise books and ran for the bus. Suddenly the square was empty. A few people were still sitting on the benches, and the man kept on sweeping. . . .

After I had rested a while my stomach reminded me I had eaten nothing this long day and wouldn't refuse some offer of food. It was late for begging — everything was closed. I picked up my knapsack and took a turn around the square but the young people hadn't left much. I did find one slice of bread, which was welcome. Rummaging through the garbage in this way I came near to the man who was sweeping. I couldn't resist approaching him. I had no idea how he would react if I attempted to engage him in conversation but, being so near now, I should at least greet him.

"Good evening, friend," I said. "The square will be very clean when you're finished."

He stopped sweeping, turned, and looked at me.

His eyes were luminous, deep, sweet. He responded in the clear voice of one who knows what he wants to say and chooses the words carefully with which to say it.

"Yes. Yes, it's necessary. The kids dirty it up so. . . . It's necessary."

"Your work is important. If you didn't do it, it would stay messy."

"Yes, it's necessary. I always do it. Every night. It's necessary."

From my knapsack I pulled out the piece of bread I had found and said, "I have this piece of bread. It's from the garbage but it's clean. Would you like part of it."

"No, I don't need it. I still have food. I don't need it."

Then he turned his back and resumed sweeping with the same care and attention as before. I watched him for a while. Our conversation, short as it was, had been the best present of my day. A great joy swept through me. In this brief encounter I had experienced something of the mystery of God. A space had been opened for a relationship to begin, man to man, equal to equal. I felt myself to be very small in his presence. His look, his words, his voice all told me that behind his outer appearance was hidden some-thing of rare beauty. What a mystery is the human being!

It was late and I was getting sleepy. I walked the streets looking for cardboard and a cozy place to sleep. I found only a small box and no place on the sidewalks that seemed welcoming. I tried several streets but none appealed to me. I returned to the square with my cardboard. Not even in the church entrance, my favorite place to sleep, could I lie down.

There was no one left in the square. The last pair of lovers had gone. The man had gone, too. It saddened me. Maybe I had had a secret hope that he would still be there, and maybe that's why I had come back. But now it was 11 o'clock, and surely by now he must have gone to wherever it was that he slept, a marquee, an abandoned house, a bit of sidewalk. . . . I sat in the square for a bit, undecided. Presently the man reappeared with cardboard under his arm and his two sacks but without the brooms. He came close, looked at my cardboard and said,

"Ah! It's good to have cardboard. It's better than concrete to lie on. Let's go sleep. I stay near here, by that store."

What an unexpected invitation! Never would I have dreamed that such a gift would be mine this night. This man, the mystery of whose being so fascinated me, was inviting me to share the night with him. I didn't hesitate for one second.

I fell in with his slow step and we came to the marquee of a store in one of the streets I had examined earlier. Then it had looked cold and uninviting, now it seemed to welcome me. Barbosa, for that was his name, was transfiguring it with his presence.

We arranged our cardboards and sat down on them. My sleepiness had vanished in the face of the joy and privilege of being here with this fascinating and mysterious Barbosa. An inner certainty was telling me,

"This night will be special. This night will be unique."

Barbosa began to take some things out of his cloth sacks. A bottle of water, a large cloth which seemed to be a rag but turned out to be his sheet, some plastic bags whose contents were a mystery. Out of one of these he pulled another sack and opened it on the cardboard. It contained rice, beans and meat. The strong acidy odor told me this food was not from today! He said quietly,

"Bread alone won't sustain you. Especially if it's only one slice. You have to eat strong food. Give me a bag."

I gave it to him and he divided the food into two equal parts, with an exactitude that I found impressive, as careful and precise as his sweeping.

"Take. You have to eat. Would you like some meal?"

And from the other plastic gag he pulled a little bag of meal.

We ate in silence. The acidy smell had disappeared and the food was sweet to the palate. It was the sweetness of sharing. . .the sweetness of brotherly love. . . .

I recalled some words from the Book of Wisdom, a wisdom that Barbosa seemed to incarnate. It is a prayer of the people of God who habitually pray when they receive food. It speaks about manna in the desert, that bread without flavor that the Israelites received each day through the goodness of the Father. Some verses read as follows:

"All this showed how lovingly you cared for your children. That food satisfied the desire of everyone who ate it; it was changed to suit each person's taste."

The manna of this night, this food coming from God knows where, was an excellent dish, whose taste no master cook could equal, no matter how many stars or ribbons.

It was a foretaste of the banquet in the heavenly kingdom. I knew at that moment that Barbosa and I were sitting at the banquet table given by "a king who prepared a marriage feast for his son." And it was Barbosa who had invited me, who had brought me into the banquet room, who had made me worthy of being there.

I didn't wish to break the silence of this holy meal.

"How happy are those who will sit down at the feast in the kingdom of God!" (Lk 14: 15) exclaimed one of the Jews after Jesus had spoken about the choice of places and of the invited (Lk 14: 7-14). Yes, happy indeed.

Just then a taxi stopped beside us. It was after midnight and, in this silent deserted street, this brusque interruption frightened me. Two men got out and came over to us. The more heavy-set of the two, whose belt could scarcely circumnavigate his middle, and who certainly hadn't gone hungry today, exclaimed loudly and jovially,

"Look! Old Barbosa found a buddy today. And he's even eating his rotten food."

Barbosa raised his head slowly and regarded him. Silently, and long. Time stopped. Then calmly, with no hint of contempt or hatred, not even of nervousness or of humiliation, he replied as a spiritual director would speak to a young disciple who did not understand the significance of an action or a word:

"He simply shared my meal. No one has ever done that before. This food is not rotten nor spoiled for him. It has all become sweet."

There followed moments of silence that seemed like an eternity. Barbosa fixed his gaze on the man, his shining visage hidden behind his beard and his dirty wig. This man seated on cardboard, without house or anything else, dirty and hungry, despised and humiliated, and another man standing, clean and well dressed, the key to his car in his hand, his belly ready to explode from so much eating. . .the excluded one, and society's darling and it was the excluded one who gave a lesson in living to the pampered one.

These moments of silence were so intense the other fellow could no longer stand it. He paid no attention to the wisdom he was just offered, not wanting to examine his own life. Instead he suddenly began to tell stories which had nothing to do with the situation at hand. It was now just chatting between friends. The taxi driver and his friend had known Barbosa for a long time and occasionally they stopped by to talk with him when they had no client. It was a good and loyal friendship even though it never came to sharing a meal.

It was already two in the morning when we lay down. I fell into deep sleep until the dawn, a peaceful sleep blessed by the presence of Barbosa. I went to sleep thinking, "What a privilege it is to be here," and I awoke with the same thought.

We went early to the square and sat on one of the benches. Barbosa then gave me good tips for my journey, directions to take, villages I would find. He warned me about the dangers of the road. He ended,

"God give you a good journey."

It was indeed a sending. . . , the wise Barbosa was sending the young pilgrim on his mission. . . .

Who is Barbosa? What is his mystery? It remains hidden in his heart. Perhaps it's not necessary that we know.

No, not necessary. What is necessary is that we be humble.

In every city there is a Barbosa who sweeps the streets that we mess up. In every human being Barbosa sweeps the place where the heart reposes. He removes from us all that soils us.

> ". . .he endured the suffering that should have been ours, the pain that we should have borne."
>
> *(Is 53: 4)*

We can only come to meet Barbosa in humility. None of us is worthy to embrace him, to kiss his hand, or even to polish his shoes. Only a heart that will see in this street sweep, so dirty and despised, so excluded from society, something more than what appears, will be able to meet him.

Paul wrote,

> ". . .be humble toward one another, always considering others better than yourselves."

(Phil 2: 3)

Street people, prophetic people

> ". . .I will pour out my spirit on everyone;
> your sons and daughters will proclaim my message;
> your old men will have dreams,
> and your young men will see visions.
> At that time I will pour out my spirit even on servants,
> both men and women."

(Joel 2: 28-29)

Joel foretold: "All will prophesy."

Now is the time to be silent, to be silent and to listen.
From the cross of the street people a prophetic word is coming to birth.
God is going to speak.

"To <u>have</u> nothing is to <u>be</u> everything."

Pirá,
Salvador

Yesterday afternoon Pirá, one of the street people with whom I sleep, drank a bit more than he should have. He didn't return to Piedade Square. His empty place in the church portico worried us.

Tired and distressed by his absence I lay down early and slept.

About one in the morning I woke up. Someone was shouting. It was Pirá. Shirtless. In his hand was a can filled with some sort of drink.

He sat down beside me, put his hand on my shoulder and said,

"Henrique, sit up. I want to talk with you."

I laid out the cardboards for us to sit comfortably and Pirá told his stories. They're always the same. I know them by heart from the many nights I had to stay awake and listen. I nodded off occasionally but he shook me awake.

"Don't go to sleep. I haven't finished."

Pirá is shirtless as he usually is when he's been drinking. And I have only the one I'm wearing. It hurts me to see him like this. He probably vomited and then cleaned himself up with his shirt and threw it in some corner. But even so. . .

Pirá was shirtless and I had only the one I was wearing. I kept my shirt and Pirá was without.

So the night passed. I listened, with as much attention as my weariness allowed, to these stories of my street companion, my father. Until daybreak!

Then, as I do every morning, I went to participate in the liturgy of the Benedictines, to offer in silence and recollection all that I had experienced and shared this night, to offer up all this suffering and pain, to intercede for all those who are addicted to alcohol and drugs. . . .

When I came out of church there was Pirá sitting on the steps begging alms.

He was wearing an attractive, colorful shirt, the kind I like.

"Pirá," I exclaimed. "What a fine shirt. I would like one like it."

Then his expression changed and he looked at me in silence. Finally, in a voice that came from the depths of his being, in that clear and confident voice that is his trademark, he said,

"What did I tell you last night?"

"But, Pirá, you told me so many things last night."

"But the most important?"

"I don't know. . . ."

Pirá respected my silence for a moment. But then accompanied by gestures and emphasizing every syllable he said,

"I'm going to tell you again. Listen carefully.

To *have. . .nothing. . . .* To have nothing. . .*is to be. . .*everything. Do you understand?

To have nothing is *to be everything*."

And then, in one single precise movement, he took off his shirt, his only shirt, and offered it to me with outstretched arm.

"You like it? It's yours!"

A dream at dawn

Messias,
Salvador

It was dark when I woke up this morning. Salvador was still asleep. The first buses were beginning their rounds; a vender of espresso was already looking for customers. Soon the paper boys would appear carrying their loads to all parts of the city.

I lay at the church door protected from the morning chill by a cardboard big enough to cover me entirely. The last stars still shone with the pale glow allowed them by the artificial lights of the city.

Pirá and our other street friends were still asleep. Only Messias was awake, sitting on his cardboard next to me. When I stirred, he looked at me and immediately asked,

"Henrique, if God were to come here right now wanting to take you with him, would you go?"

Barely awake, I needed some time to think. What a strange question, so early in the morning. This was not usual for Messias. I replied calmly,

"Look, Messias, I believe I would. But why the question?"

And then he told me the following:

"Last night I had a dream. I was walking down a road under a hot sun. There was nothing else, just the road and the sun. In the distance I saw an old man coming in my direction. He was a little old man, all full of sores. It made me nauseous to look at him. I didn't want to meet him, so I moved to the other side of the road. But when he came abreast of me, he came over to me and said,

'Messias, if you follow this road you will find what you dream for, wealth, a palace, a car, plenty. Everything you wish. But if you come with me, on this little path, I will bring you to a place that is very poor, very

127

poor. . . . Will you come with me?' "

At that moment, Henrique, I understood that the little old man was God. I took him in my arms, embraced him, weeping and said to him,

"I will. I will go with you."

That's how Isaiah described the suffering servant whose identity Jesus assumed,

> *"He had no dignity or beauty to make us take notice of him.*
> *There was nothing attractive about him, nothing that would draw us to him.*
> *We despised and rejected him, he endured suffering and pain.*
> *No one would even look at him — we ignored him as if he were nothing.*
> *But he endured the suffering that should have been ours, the pain we should have borne.*
> *We are healed by the punishment he suffered, made whole by the blows he received."*

(Is 53: 2b-5)

God in front of the church

Messias,
Salvador

This afternoon I met Messias again. It was early this morning that he told me the dream he had just had. We were seated in the square of Piedade looking at the church under whose portico we sleep.

I had spent the whole day praying, beginning with his prophetic dream. . . . Never for a moment did it leave me. Like Messias, I could think of nothing else. God reveals himself to the most poor, love's favorites. . . .

Then Mesias, tall, strong Messias, said in a low voice, his head bowed as though he were studying his bare feet:

"I didn't tell you everything this morning. I had this dream at dawn. Afterwards I couldn't fall asleep again — and then. . . , then I saw the little old man."

Messias stopped. He fell quiet. Because his head was bowed, I could not see his face, but I could imagine his expression. I put my hand on his shoulder as an invitation, in a gesture of comprehension, as though my silence were saying,

"I believe, Messias. I believe that you saw the little old man. I believe that God appeared to you."

Messias raised his head and looked at me. Tears came to his eyes. Then he spoke, rapidly emphasizing every word, giving them weight as though to convince me and himself simultaneously:

"I saw him, Henrique, truly I saw him. He was right here, exactly where we are now. He was standing and looking at us. Then slowly he crossed the street and climbed the steps of the church. He looked at us. He was here, very close. I couldn't move. He raised his eyes and looked at the church. And then he said,

'These bodies lying here, cast aside at the door of my house, are the blood shed by my Son.'

After that I didn't see him anymore."

In the darkness of the nights on the street

"The darkest hours of the night are followed by the brightness of day;
Faith, however, does not know the dark,
and the night for faith is always bright."

(Ambrose of Milan)

In the shelters of winter

São Paulo,
August, 1993

Because of the cold São Paulo winter, over fifty street people have died of exposure on São Paulo streets these past weeks. Therefore the city opened five winter shelters with a capacity of one hundred and fifty to two hundred persons each. However two hundred to three hundred crowd in every night. About fifteen hundred men and women are sheltered in them each night. But at least twice that many remain on the city's sidewalks and in its doorways. São Paulo, without remedy and without humanity has made itself the sad capital of street people.

Once a week I sleep in these shelters. The other six nights I sleep on the streets battling the cold with all the others who never will be welcomed indoors.

A night in the shelter is very stressful. On entering one has the impression of having arrived in a prisoner-of-war camp from some cruel, inhuman conflict, or in a refugee camp.

So many bodies stretched out here, heaped up beside each other. Here are both the atmosphere and the silence of death. There is only one toilet, one shower. There are no blankets, just thin mattresses over cold cement for the firstcomers and cardboard for the rest. On their faces as they enter one can read the misery that has defeated them. Famished faces, bent bodies, their whole being humiliated. Weighed down by so much suffering, most enter and lie down immediately, walled in by a silence that speaks loudly of what their hearts suffer. They lie down where they can find a space still free amid all these bodies to find the consolation of sleep, perhaps even peace.

No one speaks, neither at the entrance where each is registered by number (I am 153) nor in the bathroom line-up. And much less once lying down.

Lying among them, one of them, I spend much of the night in prayer. How can I sleep, here where suffering makes its moan in silence?

The cry and the appeal to vigilance which the prophet makes, echoes in the silence of this huge room where bodies lie on the ground.

> *"O Jerusalem, let your very walls cry out to the Lord!*
> *Let your tears flow like rivers night and day;*
> *Wear yourself out with weeping and grief!*
>
> *All through the night get up again and again to cry out to the Lord;*
> *Pour out your heart and beg him for mercy on your children —*
> *Children starving to death on every street corner."*
>
> (Lam 2: 18-19)

I reflect that in a prisoner-of-war camp or in a refugee camp, there would be some resistance, some fight in people; some desire for life, some hope, at least some bit of dream for a future. But here, all that has been killed. Where to look for a living flame in these dead eyes? For the brightness in the eye of a man tilling his own earth, gazing at his green bean field? The men here seem to be mere shadows of such as those.

In the 5 o'clock morning line-up, trembling from the cold, waiting an hour for a half-cup of coffee and two crackers, it seems to me I am standing in the vestibule of death. Total silence reigns in this line-up of two hundred men.

It's a heavy silence, imposed by a great misery, a misery too huge to be supported. This silence is born of hopes that have died. This is the silence of death.

I will need many hours of quiet this coming day, a silence born of loving contemplation, to be able to deposit in the heart of the most sweet Trinity, all this suffering, all this misery. Only God can carry it, can receive it.

I will keep on sleeping with these men in the winter shelters. How important it is to pray and to contemplate in these places! My nights will be vigils, offering up the silent cry that rises from the entrails of mother earth. Offering each of these abandoned bodies, cast aside in this place, each with its wounds, and raising them up to heaven.

"I have heard the cry of my people," said the Lord to Moses (Ex 3: 7). I know that each night our Father hears this cry, and that the Son lies down on the ground of this shelter alongside his brothers and sisters.

He, the Suffering Servant among the sufferers. . . .

The Exiles

São Paulo,
August, 1993

The drought which scourges the Northeast, accompanied by its terrible sister, famine, has its repercussions in São Paulo as well. In the face of drought and hunger, many fathers of families from the Northeast, people of the sertão, are forced to leave wives and children, fields and gardens to head for the illusory hopes of the South, of work, of bread, a corner in which to live. In the few days that I've been in São Paulo, I have met once again these heads of families, but now they are on the streets as beggars among beggars.

I had already met some of them earlier on the roads between the Northeast and the South during my journeying in May and June. Antonio for instance fleeing drought and hunger.

Whether they are still on the way here or already on the street these family men all give the same impression: they are lost. Uprooted from their land, far from their families, their culture and their faith, in a cold world of concrete and asphalt so strange to them, a world they fear and where they don't belong, a world they weren't made for, they are true exiles.

When I met Antonio in the state of Alagoas he hadn't eaten in three days. On seeing him, I knew immediately that this man was hungry: one becomes sensitive to these things when one has suffered the same privations. I told him he should beg at people's doors or in restaurants, that people are good and share gladly. He said in a trembling voice and with downcast eyes,

"I can't. I'm too ashamed."

Exiled. Antonio is exiled. He's not a peddler. Peddlers know how to adapt, how to beg. They know all the tricks for getting what they need. No, Antonio is an exile, a migrant in spite of himself. He is the innocent victim of the drought, of hunger, and of the exploitation of those who hold power, of money. Where will Antonio be today?

We travelled together for several days. I begged for both of us. We separated on the outskirts of Aracaju. He wanted to continue going south, to São Paulo. . .2,000 kilometers more. . . . Did he get there? Did he find work, he a tiller of the soil in the arid earth of the sertão, now lost in this forest of steel and concrete, in this unhuman capital? If he didn't, (and I know this well, unfortunately), if he didn't the street will welcome him with open arms. It will seize him and never again release him.

In these weeks spent among the street people of São Paulo, whether in soup lines or in the night shelters, I met street people that I had known in Salvador, Recife, or on the hot roads of the sertão. They flee the drought, only to find the cold of São Paulo, sidewalks to sleep on, unemployment, "people soup" so as not to die of hunger. They find another kind of chill here too, that of society, the anonymity of the big city where "no one talks to no one," the isolation, and for some, even despair. These are the humiliations that await them.

Antonio will be one more anonymous person among the street people, poor among the poor, rejected and humiliated. He will have lost the dignity of eating the fruit of his sweat and labor, the beans and manioc he planted, suffering instead the humiliation of beggary, and he is ashamed to beg. . . . This will be a wound in that worthy heart that will never heal.

Police violence on the street

São Paulo,
August, 1993

During this first week on São Paulo's streets, I have been accosted every day by the various police forces that watch the city center. And not always with respect, sometimes even with violence, both physical and verbal. Here for instance is the PTM, The Patrol or Tactical Mobile Police, much feared by street people. They've already arrested me twice in this short time, only because of my sleeping on the streets.

Just last night I was walking with Juan under a viaduct where we planned to sleep. . . . Suddenly two PTM cars, lights flashing, stopped in front of us. Ten police, five out of each car advanced on us, weapons at the ready, yelling,

"Hands up!! Against the wall! Spread your legs!"

There was nothing we could do but obey. There we were, then, our backs to them. Such inner tension, knowing that ten men are behind you, armed and nervous, violent in both word and gesture, and you can't see anything: you can only hear their footsteps, and you have no idea what's going to happen. With kicks to our legs they forced our feet back from the wall and examined us. They even forced us to drop our pants. Not finding weapons nor drugs they tried to convince us that we used drugs "at least once in a while". . . . We answered their questions as briefly as possible. Disappointed and furious they sent us on our way with some swift kicks to our backsides.

It bothers me that this happens daily. There are also the Metropolitan Guards and the Military Police. . . . In fact, just in the time that I wrote this letter I was ordered twice to move on. I would never think of lying down on a park bench much less in the subway. I wouldn't be there ten minutes before being ordered away. Before I sit down I look all around to see if there are guards or police. When I pass a police station, or I see a car of the Military Police or worse still of the Patrol, my hair rises in fear, knowing they could stop. . . .

The violence of the Military Police in the massacre of street children at Candelaria church in Rio de Janeiro in August of 1993 is not an isolated event. If the contact between police and the street people doesn't always end that tragically, nonetheless we feel that for the police we ought not to exist; that a street person, whether child or adult is good for nothing and ought to be eliminated. The resulting violence is simply the result of this attitude, of the formation — or deformation? — that they receive. How in these confrontations, given that meetings with them are unfortunately limited to confrontations, can one awaken in them the thought that we are people? What should be our attitude? It seems to me that keeping quiet and lowering one's head is the only way to escape with one's life, but I also think this is not a gospel response.

There where we sleep:
"A gloomy land, like the kingdom of death."

Salvador,
December, 1994

"There where we sleep". . . . It's a long story. We were expelled from the door of the church where we had been sleeping all these years.

Behold us here, then, a little farther away from the church. Even if one thinks here of church simply as the church building, still the expression is painful.

"A little farther away." But that's how our situation worsens a little more. . . .

"A little farther away" and the misery of the street people increases just a little more. . . .

A little farther away so that the sidewalk in front of the church stays a little cleaner, and we go to a place that is dirtier — just a little more. . . .

A little farther away, only so that those going to mass can do so a little more tranquilly.

A little more rejected. That's how we feel today, humiliated and reject-ed! Just a little more. . . .

Now we sleep under the marquee of a warehouse in a dark and gloomy street. The sidewalk is heaped with garbage, sewage runs open to the sky. Cockroaches and rats are our nightly companions. And that's to say noth-ing of the countless ants that run over our bodies at night as we lie on our cardboards.

It's a place of death. . . .

Our group consists of thirty persons. Most of them are already destroyed, victims of drugs, of alcohol, of prostitution, of sexual promis-cuity. . . . With us is a young man without legs, an old man with one arm missing. There are men, women, children and old folks. All of them soci-ety's rejects. . .

Our nights are filled with screams, with violence, with despair. . . .

There is Carlos for instance. When drugged with cocaine he's not the same man. He loses total control of himself. His life centers on his favorite football team, of which he is an ardent fan. But his team lost in the quarter finals, and so his life is over. There is nothing left of his hopes, his dreams. Nothing left, just this white powder.

And then there's Luciano who beats his woman every night, while she does everything she can to get even, from little provocations to big ones like urinating on him. Violence is then unleashed, uncontrollable violence. But suddenly they calm down and fall into each other's arms. After such episodes they will have sex on the sidewalk, with only a bit of cardboard giving them some privacy.

Among us is the mother of a family. Today she came back all covered with blood, knifed by another street woman. They fought on account of a doll for their daughters.

The police show up here between three and four in the morning, in the wee hours when we might get some sleep. With lights flashing and billy clubs in their hands they erupt into our night with violent aggression. They yell, wake everybody, threaten them and beat anyone who protests.

The night of nights of the street people. . . ! The darkness is so dense on the sidewalks of the big cities. The street lights are artificial and cold, deceiving and false, illusory. They cannot dissipate this kind of darkness.

Lying on the sidewalks, between cardboard and wind the darkness envelopes us.

The shadows of night. . .the inner shades of so many destroyed persons. . .the shadows of society, of rejection, of injustice. . .the darkness of exclusion.

Death surrounds us. It spies on us, awaiting its hour. Perhaps it's choosing its next victim at this moment.

The street is the place of death, not of life.

To be there during this Advent, simply to be present, poor and loved, wounded by so much suffering, so many cries in the heart of the night. . .perhaps that's part of the mystery even of Advent, the mystery of the incarnation. Jesus comes to the heart of our anxieties, to the cry of our pains, to the clamor of our miseries, in the nights of humanity.

> *"Emmanuel". . . , it means: God with us. . . .*
> *"Jesus". . . , it means: The Lord saves. . . .*

The prophet cried out:

> *"The people who walked in darkness have seen a great light;*
> *They lived in a land of shadows like those of death but now light is*
> *shining on them."*

> *(Is 9: 2)*

The light shone.
Jesus came.
Jesus is here.

That this Advent, this Christmas, we may be able to recognize him, to offer to his open arms and to his hopes, the love and tenderness that he awaits.

The "House of Jesus" and Jailza's cake

Salvador,
Christmas, 1991

Salvador, the 24th of December. . .the square of Piedade where I've been sleeping with the street people the last six weeks. It's late in the afternoon.

With a group of street children we are putting the finishing touches on "Jesus' house" for Christmas. Cardboard boxes, wooden boxes, personages painted by the children, stars cut out of "marmitex" lids. . .a house for Mary, for Joseph, for the new-born. A shelter like those we make for ourselves each night on a spot of sidewalk or in a church door. A little house where the children can rejoice as they go in and out, with a box sheathed in cloth scavenged from the garbage dump, a box in which a doll reminds us of the coming of Jesus, so poor and so humble. They rejoice in bringing him flowers gathered from here and there, filling the little house with their beauty.

The initiative came from the children themselves. One night, at an hour when the streets have emptied and are turned over to the street people I told a group of them the story of the birth of Jesus. "Manger" and "crib" are unknown words to children who know only the realities of the street. I explained that when the mother of Jesus was about to give birth, she was travelling and far from home. With Joseph, her husband, she had not found a place for the night, and it was time for the baby to be born. . . . A little girl, about twelve, didn't let me continue. She exclaimed,

"But then they have to stay on the street? Like us? But a baby can't be born on the street!"

"Yes, Silvana, you're right. But we know many mothers who have given birth on the street, right? You know, for instance, Adriana, Katia, Joelina. . . ."

"Yes, but that's not right."

Silvana fell silent for a while, thinking. Then she added,

"So, let's make a house for Jesus. For him to have a place to be born."

"What?" asked another child.

"A little house. We can find cardboard and crates and make a shelter nice and warm for Jesus to be born in. Because he can't stay on the street. . . ."

And that's how that project began, to make for Jesus what the children called "the Jesus house." It was born in that night of the city and of the street, from among the excluded. It was born in the hearts of children, out of their compassion.

This is our second "crib." The first one, made on December 21, was taken down by the police on the afternoon of the 23rd. When I came to the square that night, there was nothing left. Nenê, a boy of thirteen, came running to meet me and, embracing me, said,

"They took it down. . . , but we're going to make another one for Christmas, aren't we?"

Seated on the grass beside our rebuilt "Jesus house" a group of us were talking, among us a girl of twelve or thirteen, Jailza. Most didn't know what Christmas was. For them it was a day when people came by in cars to hand out used toys through the car windows.

"We're celebrating Jesus' coming among us. It's like celebrating his birthday," I told them.

"Jesus' birthday?? Then let's make a cake for Jesus," said Jailza.

"What a good idea, Jailza! Do you know how?"

"I do. All I need is a little water, some earth and a form."

We found these easily in our "treasury," a big cardboard box the children had found in the garbage.

It was time for vespers with the Benedictines so I left the rebuilding of the Jesus house in the children's hands and the cake-making in Jailza's. After a full day it was time to rest in Christ. I put it all in the hands of the Father and abandoned myself to the breath of the Holy Spirit: letting it all "be done" rather than "doing it."

Night had already taken possession of the city when I returned to the square. Jailza called me and took me by the hand to bring me to the baby Jesus. The children had arranged a "table" covered with a colored cloth decorated with flowers and in the center was the cake, the Jesus cake, all made according to the realities of the street: a cardboard box as table, a colored plastic bag as cover, a cake of clay and water. . .

How could one not marvel? A child's bold imagination opened for them on the street a space in the world's established traditions. Suddenly, in this opening of hearts, it seemed to me that I had never celebrated Christmas before and that a little girl was evangelizing me.

But my surprise could be only greater and the call to conversion even stronger when, after some moments of silence filled with a Presence, Jailza took my hand, exclaiming,

"And now let's eat the Jesus cake."

I was unable to hide my alarm: "What?!!"

But she ran to call the others and soon some fifty street children were seated around the table with her cake of clay and water. We inserted a piece of paper into the "cake" for a candle and lit it singing "Happy Birthday."

We had to light the "candle" frequently because so many children wanted to have the honor and fun of blowing it out.

While one girl was improvising napkins from an old newspaper, Jailza cut the cake with a piece of iron and gave each of us a piece. Everybody licked at the "cake" and pronounced it marvellous:

"How tasty!"

"What a nice birthday party."

"Can we do this again next year?"

"Don't forget to invite me."

> *"O Lord, our Lord,*
> *Your greatness is seen in all the world!*
> *Your praise reaches up to the heavens;*
> *It is sung by children and babies.*
> *It is the strength that confounds the powerful."*

(Ps 8: 1-2)

Nequinha and Junho
A message from the street for Christmas

Salvador,
Advent, 1992

The street children of Salvador did not forget the Jesus house of last year, the crib of cardboard, crates and flowers, all garnered from the garbage. A "house" to welcome Jesus, just a cardboard shelter, the same as their own.

Neguinha had been there contemplating it during the three days it stood in the square of Piedade in Salvador's upper town. She was eighteen at the time and three months pregnant with her first child. A young street girl and soon to be a mother, she meditated over the story of Christmas, over the coming of Jesus among us, and stored it in her heart. How she must have felt what Mary lived through that night.

In June, in Brazil's longest night of the year, Neguinha gave birth to her first born son. She gave her street friends the privilege of naming him and they chose "June."

At the beginning of Advent we were again seated in this same square talking about Christmas coming. The children were deciding on the best place to put the Jesus house this year and what day to build it. They were lively and full of ideas.

Neguinha was there nursing little June, silent as always. Suddenly, in a voice that was serene and self-confident, as of one who has meditated for some time on what she was about to say, she took the floor and announced,

"Yes, we are going to build it again but a lot bigger so that we can go into Jesus' house too. And little June will be Jesus because he, too, had no place to be born and came into the world poor."

"To go into Jesus' house". . . , what a lovely expression. An expression that can only come to birth in the heart of a street mother, a mother who brought a son to the light of day while having nothing, rejected everywhere, there being no place for her, a woman who had only a patch of sidewalk and a bit of cardboard. . . .

"To go into Jesus' home" — that's a cry from the heart, the wounded heart of a street mother, homeless, shelterless. It echoes in our hearts as an interrogation:

"And you, what is Christmas for you? After so many years, so many celebrations, have you already entered the house of Jesus?"

Who of us can understand the heart of Mary the way Neguinha understands it? Or understand and live Christmas as she does?

Neguinha, you are for us the door through which we can enter this great mystery of Jesus' coming, Love become a child. Only you, yes, you alone can invite us to come into Jesus' house. You, who have nothing have given us the best of Christmas presents.

Sharing in the house of Jesus

Salvador,
Christmas, 1992

Christmas! Of this night without equal, I will ever keep in my heart one of the most dramatic signs I ever saw, one of the most vivid signs of the living gospel that I have ever witnessed. It ought not to have happened, and it may never happen again, but it can save the human race.

This Christmas Eve there were two places in Piedade Square where there was an air of expectation, each specific to its place. One was the portico of Piedade church, the other, the Jesus house.

At the church door entire families from the outskirts of Salvador and some street people were waiting for the banquet crumbs of those who have too much. They come by here on Christmas Eve in their cars and throw — rather than give — what they don't themselves need. Some distribute sweets, cake, cookies, even dry crackers; some bring last year's toys to make room for this year's.

Ceaselessly the cars come by and the circus repeats itself. Each car has just a little bit and the people are many. Like a swarm of bees children, young people, adults flock to the car windows to pull out things — things they don't even recognize.

The law of might rules here. One person may come away from this night with a sack full of bread, or with three balls for his children, while others come away empty-handed. Who doesn't fight gets nothing. Solidarity and sharing are totally forgotten in this end-of-the-world spectacle, and that in front of a church, in front of God's house!

Pirá was there sitting on the steps. He lives here on the sidewalk. Christmas Eve or not, here he stays. I saw him already from far off, dejected and sad, his hands joined on his walking stick. Even though I didn't want to witness these goings-on I went to sit beside him. Pirá has never fought to get anything, that's why he's here with nothing. . . .

As we were talking, another car stopped in front of us. Right away the same race toward it. The crowd passed in front of us pushing and shoving. A little girl, about five or six was among them. Coming down the steps she fell. Right in front of us, maybe six meters away. She fell but this human sea didn't stop. Who was going to stop? They continued their desperate race in the vague hope of getting a present or a piece of cake. And they stepped on the little girl. One after the other they stepped on her. They stepped on her arms, her stomach, her legs. She turned and twisted on the ground trying to protect herself. In vain.

The human wave had hardly passed when her mother arrived, yelling. She grabbed the girl nervously, violently, blaming her for having fallen and led her to the car.

Then the crowd returned. The first half dozen were grinning, having gotten some dry bread. Dry bread for Christmas! Whoever gave it is certainly not eating dry bread tonight. The others came back bitter at not having received anything at all. Next time they'll shove harder. And the nervous, violent mother came back carrying the little girl who had fallen. She was crying. She understood nothing of what had just happened. She only knew pain, fright and tears this Christmas Eve.

Is this a society? The way we live?

A cry rises from my heart, a clamor against injustice, a demand for equality, a petition for respect. What happens at the entrance to that church is not sharing. Sharing is dividing in two what I have. It's not giving a dry piece of bread when one has roast turkey with chestnuts, chocolate cake and champagne. That's not only not sharing, but also not charity. To love my brother and my sister means to give my life, to give my time, to be ready for an encounter, a meeting of hearts and minds. Giving a dry bun through a car window and then fleeing to one's house (or mansion?) is to run away from encounter. We generate misery and hunger and afterwards tranquilize our conscience by letting these crumbs fall out of our car windows.

The crying of this little girl, victim of this false sharing, this hypocritical charity, thunders in the dark shadows of this night, this night that ought to be so bright with hope.

Pirá said, "Let's go. It's no good staying here."

In the square we found some peace. Hardly had we sat down when a boy came running. It was Luís. He had helped build the Jesus house. He was all excited and said, speaking rapidly:

"We've been looking for you everywhere! A padre came a half hour ago with a tray of sweets, there by the Jesus house. He said it's for everybody and that you should distribute it. Let's go. Everybody's waiting."

He took my hand and led me hurriedly to the Jesus house. After the apocalyptic spectacle I had witnessed at the church door I doubted there would remain so much as a crumb of what the padre had brought.

When we arrived there were over twenty street children seated on cardboard all around the "crib," lit up with candles. And in their center was this tray full of sweets. No one had as yet touched any of it. Everybody was waiting to share.

I knelt — well, more exactly, I fell to my knees, on the cardboard alongside the children. A great light shone at this moment, a light that promised hope. That light was saying, "It's Christmas!"

Nenê entoned Silent Night, his favorite, and everyone joined in. Together we thanked the Father for the tenderness of this night.

I had no wish to distribute the sweets. They were for everybody. The miracle of Christmas had to continue. So I said,

"Tonight is Christmas. It's the night of Love, the night of sharing. Seeing that you all knew how to wait to eat of this gift the padre sent, let me make a proposal. Let's say we do as follows: the tray will pass from hand to hand. Each one takes what is fair so that the last one will have just as much as all the others. Because this is Christmas and Jesus came that we all might be happy, and equal. You're OK with this?"

"Yes!" "OK."

"So, then stay seated. We're not going to line up. The tray will pass from hand to hand. Nenê, you're the closest. You take the tray and pass it to Jorginho who is the smallest. He will help himself and pass it on to his neighbor."

And it was done! I was the last to get the tray and in it were three pieces of cake, and two "saltines," the same number Jorginho had taken.

Miracle of Christmas. . .twenty-five street children, engaged in the struggle for survival, living amidst violence and drugs, accustomed to steal, came to this moment of sharing, of love.

They lived Christmas. It is gestures like these that save humanity.

The name "Jesus" means exactly this: "God saves."

House and Crib

Salvador,
Christmas, 1993

Today is Christmas. I spent this magic night and this day with the street children in the high town of Salvador, especially in the square where we slept this Advent and where we made the Jesus house.

It's already become a tradition for the street children of the city. This is the third year in a row. The three days before Christmas are dedicated to preparing this house.

This year it was even more beautiful. The creativity of the children was beyond our imagining. The chief architect was Cicero, a boy who sleeps with our group. He gave himself totally to this project during these days. This house was taller than the previous ones, built like a tent around one of the trees in the square. It was painted inside and outside with Christmas motifs and messages:

"Peace on earth," "Merry Christmas," "House of Jesus."

The children made Christmas bells out of plastic cups salvaged from the garbage of luncheonettes. Washed and painted in lively colors, they were suspended mouth downward from branches of the tree, and for the clapper each bell had a flower! So beautiful. . . . One doesn't need a lot to decorate for a celebration, just simplicity of heart. . . .

For the first time the university, on the other side of the square, made a crib. Artistically, for a certain kind of taste, it was perhaps good. It contained life-size figures clothed in real, even sumptuous clothes, with shoes waxed and shined. Its sheep were covered with wool. It had plants and trees, glass balls and Christmas garlands imported from the rich world, and all lit up with electric lights. . . . A crib behind grating, behind bars! Made to be seen, perhaps even admired. From far off. From the other side of a barrier. . . .

On the opposite side of the square the street children have not made a crib but simply a cardboard shelter. A little house, a house for Jesus. And children go into this house and come out of this house the whole day long, boys and girls of the streets. Some are shirtless because they have no clothes. Others are barefoot because they have no shoes. Some dogs, street dogs of course, go in and out with the children, sharing their joy. Some flowers, gathered by the children, God knows where, embellish the little house, and some candles. Many candles. They create living light, dancing and singing, illuminating faces and smiles.

A crib and a little house!

Life is here on the side of the little house. During the day activity never stops, even today, Christmas Day, when the center of the city is deserted after days of commotion. To make bells, to cut cardboard stars, to paint the house, to gather flowers. . .! The children never stop decorating, beautifying what belongs to them. And they play here, tell stories, sing, dance. . . .

And every night we pray together. We light the candles in the little house and everybody sits in front of them on cardboard. And there are adults present, too: Pirá, Domingos, Juçara and Miudo, and whoever may wish to pray with us. Cicero loves "Silent Night" and we have to sing it not once, but several times! It's happy prayer, lively, spontaneous. . . . It's a privileged moment with the children, an opening up to the meaning of Christmas, to our Father, to Jesus who came.

On this night, Christmas night, we stayed like this in the Jesus house until dawn. The children came and went, sometimes sleeping on our laps, faces innocent and peaceful. . . . Members of a parish came to sing with us after their Christmas mass.

It was a night of enchantment.

We ought to pray where people sleep. . . on the street

Mario, São Paulo

*"Behold the white dove returning to the arc with its green branch,
And happy the turtledove to have found its mate along the green
brooks."*

(John of the Cross)

*"Let me see your lovely face
and hear your enchanting voice."*

(Song of Songs 2: 14b)

Thus sings the lover to the well-beloved, whether in the mystic poetry of John of the Cross or in the love song of the Song of Songs.

And that's how the Beloved speaks to Messias, to Cinira, to all those who, despite their being imprisoned on the street and despite their misery have not lost the dignity of children of the Father.

These last letters highlight the spiritual life of street people, sketching their intimacy with the sweet Trinity. Just as Roberto called a little pilgrim to prayer at night, so these men and women call us to conversion.

Let us listen to them, and allow them to bring us into the mystery.

"Let me pray with you."

*Messias, Salvador
Salvador, Advent, 1992*

Some days ago a man of the street joined our group, sleeping in the entrance to the church of Piedade. He was so tall, so strong, one would think he could knock down any tree. But his heart is so tender that it immediately inspires confidence. One perceives a treasure hidden within.

Some of our group already knew him, Jacobina for example who knows everybody. I had never seen him myself except perhaps at "Chico,"

146

eating the São Francisco lunch.

His name is uncommon, and carries the promise: Messias. The "Anointed"..., who knows what his presence will bring to our group? Just his ability to create friendship is already a blessing. And his laughter brightens our nights.

The night before last, as usual, I dedicated the last moments of the waking day to prayer, the night prayer, the prayer of abandonment.... I prepared my cardboard, took out my bible, and knelt down. Beside me Pirá, faithful friend, was already sleeping. In fact, most of them were. Only Messias, a little farther away, was still sitting on his cardboard, watching the life in the square.

Then he got up and came over as if he wanted to ask me something.

"Let me pray with you," he said.

He knelt near me. The cardboard cross which keeps the night vigil while we sleep was beside the little icon of the most tender Trinity. In front of them was the open bible.

"Is this the cross of our Lord?"

"It is. He keeps watch. He guards us from the perils of the night. That way we can sleep peacefully, confident in God's protection," I explained.

"And this, what is it?" he said pointing to the icon.

I told him the story of God's visit to Abraham at Mamre, how Abraham had welcomed the three angels and had given them a meal (Gn 18). I explained that one could see in this a veiled revelation of the mystery of the Trinity, of one God in three persons.

Messias' heart, the heart of a child, was completely open. Docile, simple and innocent, he was in God's company.

After a brief silence, Messias asked:

"Read a passage from the bible."

I took up the Word of God and read slowly, praying. What passage would best suit this moment of grace? I chose the four beatitudes in Luke:

> *"Happy are you poor;*
> *the Kingdom of God is yours!*
> *Happy are you who are hungry now;*
> *you will be filled.*
> *Happy are you who weep now;*
> *you will laugh!*

Happy are you when people hate you, reject you, insult you, and say that you are evil, all because of the Son of Man! Be glad when that happens and dance for joy, because a great reward is kept for you in heaven."

(Lk 6: 20-23)

I read slowly, savoring every word, and in the ensuing silence, I let the Holy Spirit act in us. It was Messias who was able to comment on these beatitudes; he had more to teach me than I him.

Beatific silence, in which God's word comes down into our hearts and gives fruit we didn't expect and couldn't even imagine! It is in this silence that the Holy Spirit finds the free space in which to murmur to our thirsty souls the mysteries contained in the sacred text.

Messias, kneeling, eyes closed, his body leaning slightly forward, remained in deep silence. The square disappeared. The buses stopped running, the pedestrians were gone, the noise had all subsided. The artificial lights went out too, allowing the stars to shine in full glory. The flickering of a candle that didn't in fact exist, lit the icon and the face of Messias. And the icon became his face and his face became the icon.

There was only silence. Silence. . .and Messias in the heart of the Father.

Making no motion but in a firm voice, he said,

"It is for us. Jesus said this for us."

Then he got up, looked at me intently, and said,

"Thank you. Good night."

And I am obliged to you, Messias, anointed by God. . . , and may God grant you a good night.

"A bit of heaven"

Cinira, São Paulo

São Paulo,
October, 1992

The cold was severe in São Paulo these first days of September. Whoever has slept there on sidewalks or under viaducts will know. But of the three weeks that I lived with the street people in this huge city, this endless city, what I will always remember is the human warmth and love of these "street sufferers" as they call themselves.

We were a group of five to ten that met nightly to scavenge cardboard and food from the garbage. Then we would move away from the cathedral square for our evening at our "nook." Sometimes we would choose the steps of a church, or the marquee of a store or clinic. It was always a bit away from the city center, maybe three kilometers. We walked in a group, stopping here and there, talking and playing, sharing the joys and tears of the day, retelling the news, helping Djalma or Washington to walk when drunk. . . . It took us a good two hours.

But what holy hours they were! Such a fine communion we experienced, and what a feast if we found part of a pizza or the remains of a chocolate cake! It was the feast of the little ones, of those who had not eaten that day, a feast whose joy was that of the heavenly banquet.

Once at our "nook," our little sleeping corner, wrapped up in our blankets against the night cold and against this unhuman city, we covered the ground with cardboard, preparing our sleeping quarters.

But before lying down and giving brother body his merited rest, José silently and devoutly lights the candle that will burn all night. This respectful silence passes from one to another and, without anyone saying anything, we all kneel.

It is our time of prayer, our time to thank God for our day and confide to him our night on the street. It is the moment in which we give all into the hands of the Father, our "beloved Father" as José always said.

Then Cinira, Wilson and Juan would lead the group in prayer animating us with their own words, coming out of the reality of their lives on the street. A prayer like a cry to God from the heart devoid of every artifice, of every mask. Prayer that was life: naked, offered, yielded.

Most of the time I remained silent, drinking from this living fountain of faith, the faith of the poorest.

> *"You are a God who cares for the humble and helps the oppressed.*
> *You give support and protection to people who are weak and helpless.*
> *You save those who have lost hope."*

(Judith 9: 11)

All this was present here with his humiliated children: oppressed, weak, abandoned, and sometimes even desperate. And I had the privilege of being witness to this moment of love, of this dialogue of love and compassion between the "beloved Father," and his chosen children, the men and women of the street, the favorites of Love.

One night after the Our Father, sitting about our lit candle, a profound silence came over us. It was a silence born of a presence, a presence that words cannot reveal, that eyes can't see nor ears perceive but of which each of us was intensely aware. No one wanted to break this silence. Words would simply have impoverished the moment.

Christ was here.

In the cold of the night and the street, in the darkness of this city and of this world, among the rejected and excluded of our society, a light was shining. It radiated, it shone, it spread its glory. Each of us partook of this light. I believe our "nook" itself was illumined.

Then Cinira spoke in a sweet slow voice as one revealing a great secret, a pearl of great price, a hidden treasure:

"What we are experiencing now is a bit of heaven on earth."

A bit of heaven on earth. . . . It is as Jesus said,

"Happy are the pure of heart,
For they will see God."

(Mt 5: 8)

Vigil

São Paulo,
September, 1993

The cold still holds São Paulo in its grip at the end of winter. I find myself in the valley of Anhangabau, near the city center, wrapped in my too-thin blanket. The cold of dawn has penetrated to my marrow. On the bench next to me Dario is sleeping. We slept very little during this night, here at the entrance to a subway station. Alonso and Isabel, our companions of the night, had drunk too much. They did not allow the night, the restorer, to grant us its promised rest and tranquillity.

Looking at Dario lying there, given up to life-restoring sleep, I discover in him a striking beauty. Yes, this man of the streets and sidewalks of São Paulo, streets on which he has been living some twenty years, possesses a rare beauty. Is it his perpetual smile, even when asleep as now? Or his welcoming nature? The other night it was after midnight when I came to sleep. While I was rummaging quietly among my cardboards arranging them over the cold concrete, his gentle voice came from under his blankets:

"It's you, Henrique? Do you know what time it is? We were waiting up so we could pray with you, but it was getting so late, so we prayed without you. But we prayed as if you were here. So now, say your prayers and go to sleep. In the morning we plan to get up early to go to the Franciscans for breakfast. Sleep in peace."

Dario's beauty comes, without a doubt, from his child-like heart, from his purity, his innocence.

The Military Police have just been here, interrupting this letter. Armed with billy clubs, violent in word and gesture, they woke up Dario and pulled the blanket off me.

"You lazy fellows!! Asleep at this hour! You have no business being here!! Get moving! And see that it's far from here!"

I guess not everybody can see such beauty. . . .

They say here in São Paulo that we "mess up" the city squares and parks. The new mayor wants a "clean city." The message is clear: there is no room here for the street people, for the "street sufferers" in the words the homeless themselves use.

Now we are sitting on the steps near the Metro entrance. Dario has fallen asleep again. Lucky Dario. A pale sun begins to warm us a little. But I know this warmth won't last. . .in ten or twenty minutes the "black shirts," the Metro watchmen, will arrive and chase us away: "This is a public place. You can't stay here," they said to me once. But do the street people not belong to "the public?" Are they not people?

Such a denial of the human, the spiritual in the homeless.

Meanwhile we held a wake service for Cinira, celebrating her death and resurrection. I have known her for a year now, a woman of God, prophesying in both word and attitude. We held it in the place where we used to sleep, in the doorway of a clinic. There were fourteen of us spending this night in prayer, in sharing, and in silence. We made an altar from a cardboard box, the kind we scavenge each night for sleeping. We placed on it the icon of the sweet Trinity, lighted up by a candle which burned the whole night. We decorated with flowers found in the garbage of the city.

How blessed was this night! Each of us shared the most memorable of our experiences with Cinira. We shared bread too, and a banana that one of us had found.

All of us were moved but none of us was sad. Each face was lit by candlelight but radiated a light that came from elsewhere. I recalled several times what Cinira had said last year in this same place, at the conclusion of our nightly prayer:

"What we have just experienced is a bit of heaven on earth."

This vigil, too, was a bit of heaven on earth. . . . Of heaven where Cinira now lives.

Two days later I met Mario Gomes, who had taken part in our vigil and he told me confidentially,

"When are we going to hold another vigil? You know, we need to. We have to pray in the street, there where we live."

Pirá, my "father" on the streets of Salvador, once told me:

"People always give bread, a piece of bread. I don't want that anymore. Their bread is the bread of death. I want the living bread, and this bread nobody, but nobody, offers."

Are we open to this cry? Can we hear it?

Who will offer the bread of life, the "Living Bread" to Pirá, Mario Gomes, Messias, Isabel, Jacobina. . .? To all these people famished and thirsting for God?

I remember again the song of Judith. It's a song I see incarnated so often on the streets. . . .

> *"You are the God of the humble,*
> *the relief of the oppressed,*
> *the protector of the weak,*
> *the shelter of the abandoned,*
> *the savior of the despairing."*

(Judith 9: 11)

"Jesus lives in my heart"

Easter among the street sufferers

*Aracaju,
Easter, 1994*

I celebrated Easter with the street people of Aracaju, the relatively small capital of Sergipe in the Northeast.

What a privilege! How open and sensitive homeless people can be to these mysteries, mysteries from which we often remain distant.

Thanks to a small community of street people, we celebrated Holy Week in a special way. We celebrated each day with concrete gestures and symbols, filled with hope and faith.

On Holy Thursday we celebrated the Last Supper with loaves of un-fermented bread laid on a white towel spread over mats all covered with flowers — a carpet of flowers. Up to Alleluia Sunday when the joy of the Resurrection inundated us. . . , passing to there by way of Good Friday, a day of silence, of adoration around the cross, a passage from darkness to light!

What riches we were granted! All brought their lives, their sufferings and wounds, their joys and their smiles. And out of these were born words of hope, of faith, of trust.

Two such words will remain with me forever:

Antonio left his father and mother eight years ago, never sending them any news. He became a vagabond, a prisoner of the street, and finally of drugs. Two serious accidents caused him to come to his senses and think about his life. Now he's thinking of returning to his family. He was welcomed by this community after his second accident, and began to experience an inner liberation. Naturally not without struggle and apprehension. When he returns home will he be welcomed? Judged? It was on Good Friday, around the cross, when we shared something about pardon and God's love, that Antonio said slowly, very slowly:

"So then, God is Father. . . .

And his judgment is to lay his hand on our head and say tenderly

'O my son. . . , my son'. . . ."

During the Easter Vigil someone else holding a lit candle, said:

"This light lives in my hand—

It is Jesus, alive in my heart."

What a mystery! These folk of the streets, so wounded and crushed, have a sensitivity and spiritual intelligence for things hidden "to the wise and intelligent" but revealed to the "little ones." (Lk 10: 21) How well Antonio experienced and expressed what we try to understand and express in babbling words.

The street people are "the poor and humble of Yahweh," the elect and beloved of the Father. They are the incarnation today of the suffering servant of Isaiah, whose identity Jesus assumed and the apostles proclaimed (see Lk 4: 16-22 and Acts 3: 13-16). As servants they are the "light of the nations" from the prophecy of Isaiah (Is 49: 6), they, the people excluded and rejected from the bright lights of the world. . . .

It is they who will open the doors of the kingdom. They will invite us to the banquet of the Lamb's wedding feast.

> *"God purposely chose what the world considers nonsense to shame the wise, and he chose what the world considers weak in order to shame the powerful. He chose what the world looks down on and despises and thinks is nothing, in order to reduce to nothing what the world thinks is important."*
>
> *(I Cor 1: 27-28)*